SEE YOU IN COURT

by the same author

A Practical Guide to Fostering Law
Fostering Regulations, Child Care Law and the Youth Justice System
Lynn Davis
Foreword by Christopher Simmonds
ISBN 978 1 84905 092 0
eISBN 978 0 85700 273 0

The Social Worker's Guide to Children and Families Law
2nd edition
Lynn Davis
ISBN 978 1 84905 440 9
eISBN 978 0 85700 814 5

of related interest

Safeguarding Children Across Services
Messages from Research
Carolyn Davies and Harriet Ward
ISBN 978 1 84905 124 8
eISBN 978 0 85700 290 7

Vulnerable Children and the Law
International Evidence for Improving Child Welfare,
Child Protection and Children's Rights
Edited by Rosemary Sheehan, Helen Rhoades and Nicky Stanley
ISBN 978 1 84905 868 1
eISBN 978 0 85700 456 7

Social Work Reclaimed
Innovative Frameworks for Child and Family Social Work Practice
Edited by Steve Goodman and Isabelle Trowler
ISBN 978 1 84905 202 3
eISBN 978 0 85700 461 1

Social Work with Children and Families
Getting into Practice
3rd edition
Ian Butler and Caroline Hickman
ISBN 978 1 84310 598 5
eISBN 978 0 85700 556 4

SEE YOU IN COURT

A Social Worker's Guide to Presenting Evidence in Care Proceedings

SECOND EDITION

LYNN DAVIS

Jessica Kingsley *Publishers*
London and Philadelphia

Appendices 3 and 4 reproduced under the terms of the Open Government Licence v3.0.

First published in 2015
by Jessica Kingsley Publishers
73 Collier Street
London N1 9BE, UK
and
400 Market Street, Suite 400
Philadelphia, PA 19106, USA

www.jkp.com

Library of Congress Cataloging in Publication Data
Davis, Lynn, 1962- author.
See you in court : a social worker's guide to presenting evidence in care proceedings / Lynn Davis. -- Second edition.
pages cm
Includes index.
Includes bibliographical references and index.
ISBN 978-1-84905-507-9 (alk. paper)
1. Domestic relations courts--England. 2. Social courts--England. 3. Evidence, Expert--England. 4. Social workers--Legal status, laws, etc.--England. I. Title.
KD751.D38 2015
344.4203'13--dc23
2014030015

British Library Cataloguing in Publication Data
A CIP catalogue record for this book is available from the British Library

ISBN 978 1 84905 507 9
eISBN 978 0 85700 925 8
Printed and bound in Great Britain by Bell and Bain Ltd, Glasgow

Contents

Acknowledgments

I am extremely grateful to Christopher Simmonds, District Judge of the Central Family Court for his very helpful comments on the manuscript and to my editor Steve Jones for guiding me through the publishing process.

I am indebted to all the social workers, child care lawyers, judges, magistrates and Children's Guardians I have worked with over the years for all they have taught me. I am filled with admiration for the sterling work undertaken day in day out in this challenging field, largely unnoticed and unappreciated by the media or the general public.

Thanks also go to Mum, Mark and the pack for their love and support.

This book is dedicated to Timothy Robert Teichmann Davis, one of the lucky ones, born into a loving family.

Preface

This book is the product of my experience as a child care lawyer acting for local authorities, parents and children (both on direct instructions and working with Children's Guardians) as well as training social workers and others involved in the court process. I have attempted to answer the questions raised by social workers in real cases and in training courses. All of the scenarios and anecdotes are based on real cases.

It is a moment of great opportunity for social workers to claim their rightful position as experts in the newly created Family Court. I hope this practical guide will help them to do just that.

Throughout the book, to avoid repetition of he/she, I have chosen one gender or the other.

Where reference is made to the law, it is up-to-date as of 24 November 2014, so please be alert to the possibility of later changes. The law and procedure described in the book apply only to England and Wales.

Any opinions expressed are entirely my own. I take full responsibility for, and apologise for, any mistakes.

Chapter 1

Introduction

Expectations and preconceptions

Are you looking forward to going to court? Or does the very thought inspire dread? Like it or not, as a children and families social worker, you will one day end up in the witness box. You owe it to yourself (not to mention your clients) to prepare yourself as well as possible, so you can approach the experience with well-founded confidence and perform your role effectively.

Many fears about court are based on unjustified preconceptions. Courts in real life bear little resemblance to TV dramas, most of which are set in Criminal Courts, which are very different in approach from the Family Court. Many dramas are also American. In the UK advocates are not allowed to stroll around the courtroom eyeballing the witness or the jury, and rarely jump up shouting 'objection'. Sadly, few advocates look like Hollywood actors, and cases seldom turn on last-minute surprise revelations.

Social workers facing their first experience of proceedings can be overawed, even fearful of court and may expect disaster. As with anything else in life, a negative starting attitude is likely to become a self-fulfilling prophecy. Expectations of problems are often fuelled by tales of difficulties experienced by others. Usually these have been grossly magnified on the grapevine, and in any event only represent a tiny proportion of cases – 'everything went fine' is not news, 'it was a nightmare' is. Try to base your ideas on reality, not on exaggerated reports.

Why do court proceedings inspire such foreboding?

Fear of the unknown

Imagine asking someone who had never even been to the theatre to step straight onto the stage and perform in a play. Surely that would be a ridiculous idea, leading inevitably to embarrassment and disaster. Yet social workers routinely seem to be expected to give evidence the first time they ever set foot in a courtroom. Being thrown in the deep end is not usually the best way to learn to swim.

Being an effective witness is a skill which can be learned. Don't assume that it should come naturally. Excellent witnesses make it all look easy – but that is usually because they have worked hard at it.

Fear of the unknown is normal. New steps, especially important ones where you are taking responsibility for serious actions and where you feel all eyes are upon you, naturally cause apprehension. The key is to make sure you are as well prepared and supported as possible throughout the process.

Remember that the final court hearing is far from the whole story. In fact, it is only the culmination of a long process which starts with social work, a skill you already possess. Any children and families case could end up in court, so it is sensible to approach all your cases on the assumption that one day you will be explaining the case and your actions to the court. That way, you ensure that every case is carefully analysed and well recorded, decisions are clearly evidenced, procedures followed, inter-agency co-operation secured and supervision sought. Your court case is then based on solid foundations. The rest of the process essentially consists of explaining to the court the social work you have done and your department's decisions, first in writing then orally in court. The new skills to learn relate only to the rules and etiquette of the presentation to this new forum but, if your work is sound, the content is already there.

This book aims to help you understand the context of court work and the details of court proceedings, particularly in care cases. In addition, take up any training on offer and make sure you benefit as much as possible from your colleagues' experience. Find people who have had a good experience of court or who are known as effective witnesses (your legal department may have suggestions) and talk to them. There is nothing like learning from someone with first-hand experience.

Don't sit back and wait for others to help you – you are not likely to be top of their list of priorities. Don't wait until you know your case is going to court – that will be too late. Get the help you need to do your job; ask and remind – insist if necessary. Read as many court statements and reports as you can before you have to write one yourself. Don't assume, however, that they are all well written. Read them critically, noting what comes over well and what does not.[1]

Go to court as an observer before you ever have to go as a witness. Family Courts are not open to the public, but judges of the Family Court are usually happy to allow one or two professionals to observe proceedings for training purposes. Ask your colleagues or your legal advisers to let you know when a suitable case for you to observe is taking place and see if you can arrange to attend.

Whenever you are in court, be it the first or the hundredth time, watch and learn. Courts vary, and every day is different; there is always something new to absorb. What is each person's role in the process? Why are they doing what they are doing? How well are they performing their role? How effective is each witness, and why?[2] Look out for impressive witnesses and analyse what makes them persuasive – see what you can learn from them. If a witness is not so compelling, consider what made you form this view, and ask yourself what would have been more effective? How is the court reacting to what is being said – in short, what works?

Formality

The stereotypical social worker has an informal approach to life and does not welcome the constraints of formality. Like all stereotypes this may contain an element of truth, but it is far from the whole picture and you are already well used to formal occasions where there are rules of procedure and behaviour. It can even be quite comforting to work in a regulated context where you know what is expected of you.

It is true that court is a rather traditional, conservative, formal affair, although far less so in the family jurisdiction than other types of court. However, as a matter of principle, it must be right that the formality of court reflects the gravity of the decisions being taken. As long as you follow the rules and conform to the court's expectations, you can

---

1   The statement checklist in Appendix 2 might help.
2   The witness observation checklist in Appendix 5 might help.

get the job done for your child client. You will learn to find your own 'witness' persona – still yourself, but a particular version of yourself.

Artificiality

Sometimes social workers feel dissatisfied with the artificiality and theatricality of the trial system. They see advocates apparently fighting each other in court, then leaving the building chatting amicably, or they see the same lawyer arguing completely contradictory cases with equal vigour from one day to the next. They suspect that the advocates often say things they do not really believe, and this seems dishonest. It all seems like a game.

An important key to coping with the court process is understanding how the system works and what roles the other participants play, putting yourself in their shoes. The advocate is simply an expert mouthpiece for his client. It has been said that an advocate is like a hired gun – he shoots whoever he is paid to shoot and his own feelings or beliefs do not come into it. It is not a game, it is a job, and a very serious one at that.

It may be that if we were starting from scratch to design a system to determine children's futures it would not look much like our current one. Even taking into account all the recent reforms, no one pretends that our system is ideal. However, wishing it were different is like the joke response to a request for directions, 'Well, I wouldn't start from here'. The fact is that, imperfect as it may be, this is the only system we have got, and we have to work within it.

Confrontation

We are all exhorted to work in partnership with parents, and as a social worker you no doubt spend a lot of time trying to secure everyone's co-operation for the sake of the child. It can seem contradictory then to have to bring the case to the adversarial setting of the court where you and the parents are on opposing 'sides'.

In other cases you may have been walking a tightrope trying to secure the co-operation of a difficult family and fear that confrontation will jeopardise any chances of progress, or even the child's safety. However, parental hostility is never a reason to fail to take proceedings; indeed it may strengthen the need to take the case into the court arena.

The fact remains that there are some matters, such as making a care order, which lie exclusively in the power of the court. When co-operation and partnership have failed to achieve a child's protection, there is no alternative but to take proceedings.

By going to court, you inevitably bring matters to a head. Except in urgent cases, a letter before proceedings spells out in plain English what the concerns are and what has to change to avoid court action. Once the case starts, everything is evidenced in formal documentation, perhaps more starkly than before, but nothing put before the court should ever come as a surprise to the family.

Family Court cases are supposed to be heard in a non-adversarial atmosphere. Being explicit about what has happened and what has to change does not require unnecessary antagonism, certainly not on the part of the local authority. Do not feel you have to put aside your professional ethos of compassion and respect at the court door, and remember that when the case is over you still need to find a way of working with the parents and child.

Responsibility

Being the key worker taking care proceedings can be a daunting prospect, but remember that you are not alone. It is the local authority which takes proceedings, not you as an individual, and many others are involved in any court case including your lawyers and professionals from other agencies. You may be taking the lead role, but care proceedings are never dependent on just one person.

You are in court as the representative of the local authority, and are of course constrained by its procedures and policies. You need to be clearly aware of the extent of and limitations to your capacity for action and how far you can or cannot make decisions to bind the authority. In return you are protected by employment legislation, so your health and safety, for example, are your employer's concern, and the local authority is vicariously liable for any actions you take in the course of your employment, even if you are negligent. That is not to say, of course, that you can escape responsibility for your actions, which might have legal or disciplinary consequences. You also have to sleep at night, so you owe it to yourself as well as to the child to do the best job possible.

The key thing to remember is that in child protection, whether in court or outside, no action should be casual, no email sent without reflection, no remark made lightly. The important thing is to think through whatever you write, do, say or decide not to do. That way, even if others later disagree with your judgment, you can at least demonstrate your reasoning and show that you took matters seriously. Principle 4 of the Association of Chief Police Officers' 'risk principles' expresses a similar idea: 'risk decisions should…be judged by the quality of the decision making, not by the outcome'.

It is vital to ensure that all care proceedings are a team effort, including multi-agency co-operation and close liaison with your legal representatives. The fact is that child protection is an art not a science. If you were looking for an easy life, you would not have chosen to work in child protection.

McFarlane J[3] summed up the situation eloquently:

> The child protection system depends upon the skill, insight and sheer hard work of front line social workers. Underlying those key features, there is a need for social workers to feel supported and valued by the courts, the state and the general populace to a far greater degree than is normally the case. Working in overstretched teams with limited resources, social workers frequently have to make crucial decisions, with important implications on issues of child protection; often of necessity these decisions must be based upon the available information which may be inchoate or partial. There are often risks to the child flowing from every available option (risk of harm if the child stays at home, risk of emotional harm at least if the child is removed). It is said that in these situations social workers are 'damned if they do, and damned if they don't' take action. Despite these difficulties, it is my experience that very frequently social workers 'get it right' and take the right action, for the right reasons, based upon a professional and wise evaluation of the available information. Such cases sadly do not hit the headlines, or warrant lengthy scrutiny in a High Court judgment. I say 'sadly' because there is a need for successful social work, of which there are many daily examples, to be applauded and made known to the public at large.

As a social worker, you are a member of a profession which has struggled to establish its credibility. Following the Munro Report[4] and

---

3   *Re X (Emergency Protection Orders)* [2006] EWHC 510 (Fam) (High Court) at para 20.
4   The Munro Review of Child Protection: Final Report. A Child Centred System. Professor Eileen Munro, DfE 2011. Available at www.gov.uk/government/publications/munro-review-of-child-protection-final-report-a-child-centred-system, accessed on 24 November 2014..

the reform of the Family Courts, there is a momentum for change. As the President of the Family Division, Sir James Munby wrote:[5]

> One of the problems is that in recent years too many social workers have come to feel undervalued, disempowered and de-skilled. In part at least this is an unhappy consequence of the way in which care proceedings have come to be dealt with by the courts. If the revised Public Law Outline is properly implemented one of its outcomes will, I hope, be to re-position social workers as trusted professionals playing the central role in care proceedings which too often of late has been overshadowed by our unnecessary use of and reliance upon other experts.

It is a moment of opportunity for social workers to step forward and live up to the expectations placed on the profession by competently presenting high-quality work. But this is a once in a lifetime opportunity to change perceptions of an entire profession. If it is missed, it will not come again.

Positives

Some social workers positively enjoy going to court and many others take this part of their role in their stride. Preparing a case and taking it to court is a stimulating intellectual challenge. It involves the rigorous analysis of facts set against legal criteria. You have the opportunity to explain and justify your professional judgment to an independent adjudicator, while countering challenges and objections.

Court work gives you the opportunity for authoritative validation of your practice and your department's planning for the child. Often judges and magistrates comment on the work undertaken or evidence given and this can include compliments on the quality of social work witnesses.

It is another step in your professional development, and achieving another milestone should be satisfying, especially if it involves overcoming difficulties on the way.

Only the court can move matters along for the child by making necessary orders, and it must be right as a matter of principle that these vital decisions should only be made after due process. The parents

---

5   'The View from the President's Chambers (2) – The process of reform: the revised PLO and the local authority', [2013], pp.6–7, available at www.judiciary.gov.uk/publications/view-from-presidents-chambers/, accessed on 3 September, 2014.

and the child himself, whether immediately if he is old enough or later when he is trying to understand his life story, have the right to know that the case has been properly thought through, scrutinised and tested.

At the end of the process, achieving the right outcome for the child makes all the difficulties along the way worthwhile.

QUESTIONS FOR REFLECTION

- How do you feel about court work? Why? Are your feelings based on fact or preconceptions?

- What do you need to do to prepare yourself for a court case?

- How can you ensure that your practice in every case could withstand court scrutiny?

Chapter 2

The Legal Context

The adversarial system

Traditionally, English courts followed a strictly adversarial model: two sides battling it out, with the court hearing each and determining the victor. The court did not dictate how the respective parties put their case, it just acted as a referee and adjudicator. Its role was passive; the court was dependent on the information brought to it by the parties themselves.

In family proceedings, the adversarial model has been adapted. The ethos of the proceedings is said to be non-adversarial, so the court atmosphere is less antagonistic than that in criminal cases, for example. In terms of procedure, the Family Court takes a more active role than a traditional court. As Wall LJ said:[1]

> Care proceedings are only quasi-adversarial. There is a powerful inquisitorial element. But above all, they are proceedings in which the court and the local authority should both be striving to achieve an order which is in the best interests of the child.

The court controls case management, ordering the filing of evidence from the parties, determining whether and, if so, which expert evidence can be produced and setting the timetable for the case. Court rules and procedures set out documents to be filed and the information required to be covered in social work statements. In care proceedings and some other children's cases, a Children's Guardian (see Chapter 3) is appointed to give the court a professional view, independent of the primary parties (the local authority and parents in the case of care proceedings).

---

1 *Re S & W* [2007] EWCA Civ 232 (Court of Appeal) paras 35–8.

However, it is still up to the parties to decide how to put their case. The court does not actively investigate the case or seek out information itself. It has no independent knowledge of the case, the Family Judge will never visit the family home, or see the parents interact with the child and may not ever meet the child (see pages 55–6 for more information). So the court depends on you to provide all the necessary information. If you do not tell the court something significant, it may never know. Remembering this will help you decide what information to include in your evidence.

Also bear in mind that even experienced Family Judges are not social workers and do not have the same skills as you do, for example, in interpreting family dynamics. So, as well as giving the court information, you also need to bring to the court the benefit of your expertise.

Court hierarchy

Courts are organised in a hierarchy, as illustrated in Figure 2.1, and those at the bottom of the chart are the workhorses of the system. There are two main branches of the court system – criminal and civil – which unite at the higher levels. Family cases are part of the civil side of the law.

The Magistrates' Court is the foundation of the Criminal Court system. All criminal cases start there, for both adults and young people (in the Youth Court), and although serious cases are committed to the Crown Court, magistrates deal with 90 per cent of criminal cases from start to finish.

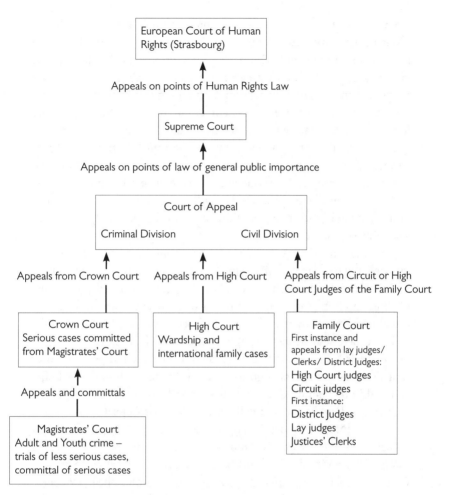

Figure 2.1 Court hierarchy in England and Wales

Family Court

The Crime and Courts Act 2013 (implemented in April 2014) changed the Family Court system. There is still a residual High Court jurisdiction for some very particular cases such as wardship and some cases with an international element but now the majority of family cases are dealt with by the single Family Court. It deals with family cases including care proceedings, emergency protection orders, contact applications and private law disputes. The three tiers of court under the old system – Family Proceedings Court (FPC), County Court and High

Court – have been united into the single Family Court. The different levels of judiciary now all sit in the Family Court with the collective title 'Judges of the Family Court'. So if you go to court in a family case you may appear before a panel of two or three lay judges, a District Judge, a Circuit Judge or a High Court Judge. Whereas in the past cases had to be transferred up (or sometimes down) to the appropriate level of court to deal with the nature of the case, now it is simply a question of allocating the case within the same court according to various criteria, the most important of which is the complexity of the case. Thus a case of general neglect – inadequate food, poor hygiene and so on – might be ideal for lay judges, but a case of an allegedly non-accidental head injury would need a professional judge, possibly at High Court level.

At the end of a case, when the court announces its decision, the unsuccessful party may wish to appeal. However, simply being unhappy with the court's decision is not enough – the aggrieved party must establish grounds for appeal, showing that the court which made the initial decision (known as the 'court of first instance') made a mistake of law, or applied the law wrongly to the facts of the case.

Appeals from decisions of a Justices' Clerk, lay judges or District Judge of the Family Court go to a Circuit Judge or High Court Judge still within the Family Court, whereas appeals from decisions made by a Circuit or High Court Judge lie in the Court of Appeal.

The ultimate domestic appeal court is the Supreme Court (which took over from the House of Lords as the highest court in the jurisdiction in October 2009). The Court of Appeal and Supreme Court are exclusively appellate courts and do not re-hear evidence, so no witnesses are called; instead they work from transcripts of the evidence and judgments given in the court below, and hear arguments on points of law. If one of your cases goes to appeal, you will not have to give evidence, so your role is limited to helping your legal team to put the case as clearly and forcefully as possible.

The Supreme Court only hears cases raising an issue of general public importance, of significance far beyond the interests of the parties involved. This totals less than a hundred cases a year over the whole range of law, so very few children's cases proceed to this level.

Once domestic remedies have been exhausted, there is the (very remote) possibility of a further appeal on questions of human rights to the European Court of Human Rights in Strasbourg.

Facts and law

A court's job is two-fold: first to determine what happened, which involves the court choosing between two or more conflicting versions of events, and second to apply the law to those facts. Constructing a care proceedings case therefore involves not just presenting the facts of the case but also establishing how the law applies to that evidence. As a social worker, you need to work closely with your lawyers to ensure that the relevant legal grounds are established by the evidence. Your advocate's job includes making submissions to the court on points of legal interpretation and, if the decision goes against you, considering whether there are any legal grounds for appeal.

Sources of law

You should be familiar with statutes such as the Children Act 1989, which is central to care proceedings. However, English law is founded on case law as well as statute. Some important doctrines of our law are purely judge-made common law. For example, the law of negligence, the cause of today's concerns about a 'compensation culture', all stems from the 1932 case of a decomposing snail found in a bottle of ginger beer (*Donoghue v Stevenson* [1932] UKHL 100).

Case law also helps us to interpret statutes as judges decide on the precise meaning of the words used in an Act of Parliament. For example, s31 Children Act 1989 defines the 'threshold criteria' grounds for a care or supervision order. Almost every word of that section has been subject to judicial scrutiny, including the small and apparently unremarkable word 'is' in the phrase 'the child is suffering …significant harm'. You might think that what 'is' means is obvious, but nothing is beyond argument to lawyers. The issue went all the way to the House of Lords (the highest court in the land at the time), which decided[2] that the court must look back at the child's situation when protective measures started, not at the time of the hearing – so their Lordships effectively decided that 'is' means 'was'.

Decisions of the Supreme Court (and previous decisions of the House of Lords) constitute 'binding precedent' setting the law for all other courts. Thus the meaning of 'is' in s31 is now decided and is not open to any other interpretation. The Court of Appeal also sets precedents for all courts below it in the hierarchy. In this way, decided

---

2   *Re M (a minor) (Care order: threshold criteria)* [1994] 2FLR 557 (House of Lords).

cases are authority for propositions of law, so lawyers on each side scour the law reports for precedents supporting their arguments. They also try to undermine the arguments put forward by the opposition by contending, for example, that a case law precedent in fact does not apply because a distinction can be drawn between that case and the matter before the court.

Lawyers usually put their legal arguments in written submissions or skeleton arguments. If you are the key worker in a case, always ask to see your own advocate's written submissions before they are handed in, so you can see how your case is put. You should also see the other parties' arguments as soon as they are received.

Another key consideration for all courts is the Human Rights Act 1998.[3] All statutes must be interpreted in a way which is consistent with human rights, and case law from the European Court of Human Rights in Strasbourg is regularly cited in our own courts. Human rights issues include the right to family life, right to a fair hearing and the right to protection from ill-treatment, so you can expect these to be raised in all of your cases.

Criminal and civil proceedings

In our legal system, cases are categorised as either criminal or civil. The criminal law defines and marks the limit of acceptable behaviour in society and an individual who steps beyond that boundary is subject to the State's censure. For this reason, prosecutions are taken in the name of the Crown, so a case against Mr Smith is called *R* (which stands for Regina) *v Smith*, and the prosecuting authority is the Crown Prosecution Service. The spotlight of a criminal case falls on the behaviour of a particular person, the defendant, and the State's job is to establish whether this individual has transgressed against a specified law, and the court acquits or convicts and punishes him.

Criminal offences are tightly defined and the prosecution must establish that each element of the offence was committed by the particular defendant on trial. He, of course, is innocent until proved guilty, an ancient protection for the individual now also enshrined in the European Convention on Human Rights.

---

3   For more information on the Human Rights Act and other elements of child care law *see* the author's book *A Social Worker's Guide to Children Law*, 2nd edn. London: Jessica Kingsley, 2014. For a brief summary of key legal provisions in care proceedings see Appendix 1.

The burden placed on the prosecution is a heavy one – proof beyond reasonable doubt is required – and the rules of evidence are strict. As a matter of principle, it is generally thought better that a guilty man go free than an innocent man be convicted.

Lay people play a vital role in the Criminal Courts. Most cases are tried by magistrates who have no legal qualifications (although they are advised by a legally qualified Justices' Clerk). In the Crown Court, where serious crimes are tried, the verdict of guilty or not guilty is given by a jury of lay people. These roles for 'ordinary people' reflect the fact that the criminal law is there to impose and enforce society's norms. This is reinforced by the fact that, except for cases against young people, criminal trials are open to press and public so that justice can be seen to be done.

Civil law, on the other hand, primarily deals with resolving disputes between individuals. Although care proceedings are classed as public law as the applicant is the local authority, an arm of the State, they still fall within the court's civil jurisdiction.

Civil courts from the Small Claims Court (part of the County Court) to the High Court are occupied with matters such as negligence claims, contract disputes and, of course, family law. Issues tend to be broader than the tightly defined offences before the Criminal Courts. The court's objective in a civil case is to resolve the dispute by making findings of fact and determining rights and duties between individuals. The court then finds a suitable solution to the problem, be it compensation, an injunction or, in family cases, an order regulating arrangements such as with whom a child lives or who she sees. Even if the court does make findings of fact (for example, as to who sexually abused the child), these do not have the same force or status as a criminal conviction and do not lead to punishment or entry on the sex offenders' register.

As a result of the civil law's function it is not necessary, nor would it be practical, for matters to be proved to the same level as a criminal case. The applicant has to establish his case 'on the balance of probabilities'; that is to say to show that his case is more likely than not to be the correct one.

Standard of proof

It is important to be keenly aware of the difference between the criminal and civil standards of proof. If these were to be expressed in numerical terms, where would you place each standard ('beyond reasonable doubt' and 'on the balance of probabilities') on a scale of 1 to 100, where 50 is evenly balanced?

Clearly the criminal standard is high, although the word 'reasonable' means that the prosecution does not have to prove its case beyond any doubt at all; 100 per cent certainty is impossible in the real world. Police officers generally put the figure at around the 90 per cent mark; still a very high level of proof.

In contrast, the civil standard might technically correctly be expressed as 51 per cent – in theory anything above 50 per cent reaches the target. However, in practice such small differences are impossible to detect and civil lawyers tend to express the figure as more like 60 per cent.

The gap between the two standards is striking; proof at a level of 75 per cent, for example, would be ample to satisfy the civil standard but would be nowhere near approaching the criminal standard.

Terminology

You need to be very clear whether you are working in the criminal or civil arena, and to adjust your approach and use the correct terminology accordingly. For example, the term 'prosecution' is only used in the Criminal Courts – to use it in care proceedings would reveal a misunderstanding and demonstrate a completely inappropriate mindset. Some differences are more subtle; for example, what we would call in the criminal context a 'confession' becomes an 'admission' in the civil court.

Children's cases

Child protection cases can give rise to both criminal and civil proceedings, meaning that as a social worker you may be required to give evidence in both the family and the Criminal Courts. Although the same basic facts lead to both court cases, your role changes from applicant in the former to witness in the latter, the respective courts vary in focus, function and approach and the potential outcomes are quite different in nature.

Sexual abuse: crime and care

Amy, aged eight, says her stepfather Barry sexually assaulted her. Police and social workers investigate, making a video-recorded interview conducted under the 'Achieving Best Evidence'[4] guidelines. Professionals agree that Amy's disclosure is clear. Barry is arrested, charged with sexual assault and taken before the Criminal Court. Amy's mother, Carrie, refuses to believe the allegations and supports her husband. The local authority takes care proceedings to remove Amy from home. Two separate court cases are underway. The Criminal Court focuses on Barry and the alleged offence; the Family Court focuses on Amy's welfare, looking at her whole circumstances, not just the issue of sexual abuse. In the criminal case, Amy has to go to court to be cross-examined, albeit via live TV link. In the care proceedings, professionals give Amy's evidence for her, and she is extremely unlikely to have to go to court to give evidence herself.

In the event, the evidence against Barry is not strong enough to sustain a conviction for sexual assault and he is acquitted of criminal charges. However, in the care proceedings the judge makes a finding that Barry did sexually abuse Amy and makes a care order.

QUESTIONS FOR REFLECTION

- How can Barry make sense of his situation? As far as he is concerned, he has been found innocent by one court but condemned by another.

- How can you explain the situation to Amy?

This table summarises some differences between the two sets of proceedings in Amy's case.

---

4   *Achieving Best Evidence in Criminal Proceedings: Guidance on interviewing victims and witnesses, and guidance on using special measures.* Ministry of Justice 2011, available at www.justice. gov.uk/downloads/victims-and-witnesses/vulnerable-witnesses/achieving-best-evidence-criminal-proceedings.pdf, accessed on 25 August 2014.

Table 2.1 Differences between criminal and care proceedings

	Criminal	Care
Parties	Crown (prosecution) Barry (defendant)	Local authority (applicant) Carrie, Amy's father (if he has parental responsibility), Amy (via her Children's Guardian) (respondents) [Note: Barry, as Amy's stepfather, is not automatically a party]
Court	Start in Magistrates' Court, committal to Crown Court	Family Court (allocated to the appropriate level of judiciary)
Decision maker	Crown Court – jury decides facts, judge determines questions of law and decides on sentencing (if conviction)	Family Court judge decides on fact and law
Privacy?	No – Crown Court open to public and press	Proceedings not open to the public; media access allowed subject to limitations on reporting
Burden of proof	Prosecution	Applicant
Standard of proof	Beyond reasonable doubt	Balance of probabilities
Evidential rules	Very strict	Less strict (for example, hearsay is admissible)
Relevant evidence	Alleged offence only	Amy's whole circumstances, not just alleged abuse
Amy's evidence	Amy gives evidence via video (evidence in chief) and TV link (cross-examination)	Video shown; interviewers give evidence; Amy extremely unlikely to come to court to give evidence
Amy's status	Victim/witness	Subject of proceedings
Focus on	Barry	Amy
Dress	Judge and advocates wear wigs and gowns	No wigs or gowns
Tone	Adversarial	Non-adversarial
Outcome	Verdict – guilty/not guilty	Decision/judgment – findings of fact
	Punishment if convicted	Order or no order – resolution of Amy's situation
Overall purpose	To determine Barry's guilt or innocence	To determine Amy's best interests

Out of control: crime and care

Donna is 14 and out of control. She truants from school, takes drugs, drinks to excess and is promiscuous. She steals to finance her drug habit. Donna is arrested, charged and prosecuted in the Youth Court for theft. She is also subject to care proceedings as she is suffering significant harm because of her own behaviour and is beyond parental control.

Both cases centre on Donna, but the criminal case concerns only her alleged criminal offences – the underlying causes and her other problems only become relevant if she is convicted and the court has to consider what sentence to impose. In contrast, the whole focus of the care proceedings is on whether Donna is suffering significant harm, and her welfare is the court's paramount consideration. In the Youth Court, Donna is the object of censure; in the Family Court she is the subject of concern.

QUESTION FOR REFLECTION

- How can you help Donna to understand why her behaviour is condemned by one court and the subject of concern for the other?

Vulnerable victims

Fred is well-known to police and social workers. They strongly suspect that he is a paedophile but they have insufficient proof. They suspect that Fred cynically chooses his victims carefully, selecting children who are for one reason or another unlikely to be able to give credible evidence (for example, they are too young, or are disabled children with communication or cognitive difficulties). When challenged, Fred denies everything and tells the authorities to 'prove it'. Social workers may be able to protect children who may be in danger from Fred (for example, if he moves into their home) but with inadequate evidence, police cannot prosecute.

Child injury: crime and care

Edward suffers physical injuries and medical opinion is clear that these were inflicted, not accidental. Evidence shows they occurred when Edward was in the care of both parents. They deny doing, seeing or hearing anything untoward but have no explanation for the injuries. There are no other witnesses to what occurred. The evidence cannot clearly establish who is responsible. What implications does this have for the Criminal and Family Courts?

Edward has been harmed; you might feel that the perpetrator should be punished. But this scenario presents an impossible dilemma for the criminal law: who can be charged? There are two suspects equally in the frame and no evidence to establish which of them was responsible – if both continue to deny everything and no other evidence is discovered, there is no hope of proving beyond reasonable doubt who injured Edward. Criminal law requires a defendant – two people cannot generally be prosecuted on an 'either/or' basis. The exception to this is if Edward dies of his injuries or if those injuries are serious, in which case there is a specific offence of 'causing or allowing'[5] death or serious physical harm to a child.

Things are different in the Family Court. It may be possible to identify a perpetrator and for a finding to be made in view of the lower standard of proof and more flexible rules of evidence. But even if it remains impossible to make a finding as to who hurt Edward, the threshold criteria[6] in care proceedings can nevertheless be satisfied (as he has suffered significant harm attributable to inadequate care) and the Family Court can make a care order if that is the right thing to do. A child can still be protected even if it is not possible to identify who harmed him.[7]

Contrast between criminal verdicts and care findings

Hedley J gave a lucid analysis of the differences between criminal and family hearings in a care case[8] where a father had been acquitted in the Crown Court of murdering one of his children. Hedley J explained that the acquittal meant that the jury:

---

5   s5 Domestic Violence Crime and Victims Act 2004, as amended.
6   See Appendix 1 for a brief definition of threshold criteria.
7   *Lancashire County Council v B* [2001] 1FLR 583 (House of Lords).
8   *A Local Authority v S, W & T (by his Guardian)* [2004] 2FLR 129, High Court Family Division, pp.6–8.

decided that they were not sure: no more than that can be read into the verdict. They may have decided that he was in fact innocent or they may have decided that he was very probably guilty but that they could not be sure of it. We do not know... In family proceedings, however, the judge's task is quite different. In the end I will have to decide whether the surviving child T can be safely returned to one or both of her parents. In order to decide that, I need to reach views about why X died and the question I have to ask is this: what was the most probable cause of her death? That is very different to the question faced by the jury both in terms of its emphasis (they were primarily concerned with the defendant whilst I am primarily concerned with the child) and in terms of the standard of proof. They had to be sure of guilt; I have to determine the probabilities and give detailed reasons for my view. Moreover I have heard a much wider range of evidence than would have been admissible in the criminal trial. It will be apparent then, however odd it may seem at first blush, that I could give a different answer to the one given by the jury yet both of us could have correctly answered the questions actually posed to us. Truth is an absolute but elusive concept and the law, in recognising that, deals with it in terms of what can be proved. The fact that something cannot be proved does not mean it did not happen but only that it cannot be proved to the requisite standard that it did. That is the price society has to pay for human fallibility in the quest for truth.

QUESTIONS FOR REFLECTION

- How do you feel when no one is prosecuted or punished for harming children, even if you are able to protect the child? How do you manage your emotions? How does that affect your ongoing work with the family?

- If, as professionals, we sometimes find it difficult to accept the consequences of the differences between the Criminal and Family Court systems, how can you explain this to children and their families?

Care proceedings: a special case

Is there ever a winner?

Although a social worker would not start proceedings unless absolutely convinced that the child needed protection, there is often a sense of failure that things have reached that stage at all, as everyone will have worked long and hard to keep the child with the family. When the local authority gets the order it seeks there may be a sense of satisfaction, but never triumph, as there usually is for the victor in other types of court proceedings.

The whole truth

In most court cases, the applicant goes all out to win, putting his case as strongly as possible and presenting only those selected facts which suit his argument. You would be surprised to hear someone suing for damages for a car accident volunteering that he himself is a bad driver, was going too fast and acknowledging that the other driver did his best to stop in time. Yet, in care proceedings, the local authority applicant effectively has to do just that. As an arm of the State seeking a Draconian order, it has a duty to put the case in a fair and balanced way, pointing out all the facts and considerations which may go against it at the same time as trying to make out its case and secure the order it seeks. As Hollings J said:[9]

> I cannot emphasise too much that applicants such as a local authority responsible for children in their care...should not act in a one hundred percent adversarial way. They must present [the case] in a balanced way and not fail to refer, it seems deliberately, to factors which point in a direction opposite to that which is desired by the local authority.

So as well as detailing in your evidence all the concerns about the child and family, you therefore also have a duty to point out the parents' love for the child, outline positive aspects of their parenting and acknowledge weaknesses in your own department's response, perhaps that you should have done more to help or should have acted sooner. In this way you provide the court with the proper information to make a decision in the child's best interests.

Multiple parties

Most court cases involve two parties – prosecution and defence, or applicant and respondent. However, in care proceedings, there are multiple parties, each of which argues the case from a different perspective.

---

9   *Re B* [1994] 1 FCR 471 (High Court).

The local authority is the applicant and there could be several respondents:

- the child's mother

- the child, represented by a Children's Guardian and a solicitor

- the father if he has parental responsibility or, if not, if the court makes him a party

- anyone else who has a separate case to make and is made a party by the court (such as family members who are applying for an order to care for the child).

Children always have a Guardian and a solicitor. For younger children, it is the Guardian who instructs the solicitor, but if the child is competent to do so, she instructs the solicitor herself and the Guardian has to represent herself or find another solicitor.

In cases involving more than one child, there may be more than one father, each of whom could be a party and separately represented.

Flexible evidential rules

Because care proceedings focus on the child's welfare, the court rules allow greater flexibility of evidence than for other categories of case (see Chapter 4). Whereas in criminal trials defence lawyers argue every technicality and plead every point, in care cases such tactics do not impress. The combative advocacy in the Crown Court might sway the jury, but the Family Court would frown on the same techniques, demanding a less adversarial approach.

Privacy

Unlike Criminal Courts, Family Courts are not open to the public. However, in recent years there has been a move against the previous rule of absolute confidentiality, which was portrayed as secrecy (which sounds much more sinister) and risked undermining public confidence in the family justice system. Now, accredited representatives of the media are allowed to be present in family proceedings, subject to the court's discretion to exclude them; for example, to protect the child's welfare or to protect a vulnerable witness. However, the media cannot see documents filed in the proceedings and they cannot report on the proceedings except with the court's permission. There is now a presumption that an anonymised version of the judgment will be published, but this is subject to the court weighing up all of the relevant considerations – permission to publish can be refused.

If publication is authorised, the children's identity must be protected (the same does not apply to professional witnesses including social workers). Protecting the child's identity is not as easy as it sounds. Simply removing names is not enough, as indirect identification is also prohibited – this includes guarding against 'jigsaw' identification, where the child's identity can be discerned by putting together several apparently innocuous pieces of information. Of course, the ability of other parties to publish information on social media is another concern. Any publicity of proceedings can have profound implications for the child concerned and you should not hesitate to raise this complex issue with your legal team.

Continuing relationships

In most court cases, the parties never have to see each other again after the trial is over. When care proceedings are finished, the judge, lawyers and Guardian all go away, leaving you as social worker to carry on working with the child and family in the aftermath of the court's decision. This has important implications for the way you work with the family before the proceedings and how the case is presented. In general, workers who are honest and clear with families throughout fare much better than those who tread too softly and do not confront issues as they arise. Families can feel betrayed by a worker they thought was 'on their side' who then stands in court spelling out their failings in graphic detail. Equally, some sensitivity is required and being frank about problems does not mean they have to be cruelly expressed – remember you have to carry on after the court proceedings are over.

QUESTIONS FOR REFLECTION:

- How can you prepare yourself for the special characteristics of care cases?

- How can you ensure that media access to the Family Court does not compromise the child's right to confidentiality?

Chapter 3

Who's Who

Parties to the proceedings

Party status is an important concept. Only the parties to the proceedings have the automatic right to receive all the papers, to attend all the hearings, to be represented by a lawyer and to put their case by presenting evidence, challenging evidence submitted by others and making legal submissions to the court. Court rules prescribe who is a party depending on the type of case. In care proceedings, the automatic parties are the local authority (applicant), parents with parental responsibility (PR) and the child (respondents). The court can join other people as parties to the proceedings.

The local authority's lawyer

The relationship between the social worker and the local authority's legal adviser (whether an in-house legal team or a contracted-out private firm) is crucial, but is often not given sufficient priority. Social workers and lawyers are professionals from different fields who should bring their particular skills to the same challenge in a spirit of mutual trust, confidence and respect, working as a team to the same end. There should be constructive criticism on both sides – far better to have tough questions and challenges posed by someone on your side when you still have time to work out the answers than to be surprised by the opposing party raising matters which should have been dealt with before.

Remember that your lawyer is just that – a lawyer, not a social worker, and has a different set of competences and skills from you. Legal training is academic, intellectual and analytical. Words are the tools of the lawyer's trade, and lawyers tend to be precise, even pedantic and they should pay great attention to detail.

If your lawyer is experienced in child care work, he may have acquired some knowledge of social work along the way, but he does not have your expertise, and you may need to explain elements of your concerns or analysis to him. Nor will he ever know the particular child or family so he depends on your 'hands on' work with the family, the factual evidence you provide and the professional skill you apply in interpreting the situation.

Expect to be challenged by your lawyer. He should ask you to explain your actions and why, for example, you provided one service rather than another. He should expect you to explain your views and justify your recommendations. He should point out weaknesses and problems to you and tell you where others will attack. Sometimes this feels dispiriting; you might even feel as if he is not on your side. Far from it – in fact, you should be more concerned if your lawyer uncritically accepts everything you say, because you can be sure that the other parties won't!

However, don't be in awe of your lawyer. Teamwork goes both ways. Feel free to ask questions, request explanations, challenge, and to put forward your own ideas and suggestions.

The lawyer's job is to advise you on the law and legal procedure, together with the strategy and tactics for presenting the case. He applies the relevant legislation and case law to the factual information and professional judgments you give him. Make sure you give him all the relevant information, and give it to him straight. Never try to put a favourable gloss on things, skirt around potential problems or miss out difficult issues – he will not thank you if something later comes to light for which he has had no time to prepare. Your communications with him are like a confessional, thanks to 'legal professional privilege' – no one else (not even the Children's Guardian) is ever entitled to know what is discussed between lawyer and client or what advice the lawyer gives, so there is no reason for discussions to be anything other than frank, open and honest.

Do you have to follow your lawyer's advice? To the eternal frustration of lawyers, the answer is 'no'. No client is ever bound to take their lawyer's advice, however forcefully given. The lawyer advises, but the client instructs. Lawyers often find themselves having to argue as convincingly and energetically as possible a case or a point they advised their clients not to touch, and in which they themselves have no confidence whatsoever. One rare exception to the obligation to follow instructions is when those instructions conflict with the duty which all lawyers have to the court. A solicitor could not, for example, agree to suppress a piece of evidence which might exonerate the parents, or put forward to the court as true information he knows to be false. He cannot breach your client confidentiality by telling the other parties or the court of your intended deception, but ethically cannot continue to act for you on that basis.

Whatever the lawyer's advice, the decision whether or not to commence care proceedings is the responsibility of the local authority and no one else – not the lawyer, Case Conference, partner agencies or any individual social worker. The local authority is the client and instructs the legal adviser; it is a lawyer/client relationship just like any other.

However, if differences arise between you and the lawyers, remember that you are just a representative of the local authority, you are not the client yourself and do not have the authority to go against legal advice. You must take matters up the line of seniority within your department to resolve the problem, following your authority's procedures for such cases.

How involved should your lawyer be in case preparation? This may be affected by limited resources, but investment at the earliest stages pays dividends later on. The procedural rules set out in the Public Law Outline (PLO) require the local authority to hold a legal planning meeting between social workers and lawyers before deciding to issue proceedings, and the lawyer should also be involved in drafting a letter before proceedings and in a meeting with the parents and their lawyers before the case goes to court. This should be just the start of a close working relationship with regular liaison and face-to-face meetings before each important stage in the proceedings.

If you do not feel you are getting the advice and support you need, say so and ask for help. Particularly when you are inexperienced in court work, it is unreasonable for your authority to expect you to work unsupported. We should never forget that these proceedings could determine a child's whole future; they deserve proper preparation.

The authority's lawyers should always be involved in preparing the evidence submitted in support of the case. As a social worker, you should write your own statement, but it should always be closely checked by the lawyer before it is finalised and distributed. In some authorities senior social workers rather than lawyers are supposed to check statements. However senior they may be, their training, experience and perspective is different and with the best will in the world they cannot do a lawyer's job. Any self-respecting lawyer should be extremely unhappy about having to present a case in which he had no input in the preparation of the key evidence. The High Court was clear[1] that statements should be prepared by someone with proper understanding of relevant legal principles, issues in the case and court procedures who should examine all background materials and files and consider what further information or material should be obtained. In that case, a 13-day court hearing took place before evidence came to light forcing the local authority to drop allegations of sexual abuse. Quite apart from the stress that must have caused to all involved, imagine how much money was wasted.

Often you will find that the person you liaise with throughout the preparatory stages does not present the case in court; instead the hearing is handled by a specialist advocate, often a barrister. There can be many reasons for this. Perhaps your legal adviser feels she has insufficient expertise in advocacy, which is a different skill from case preparation; maybe there are specific features of the case that require a specialist or she may simply not be able to spare several days in court and out of the office. The choice of the right advocate for the case is an important one. Naturally, he should specialise in care proceedings, but beyond that, factors include the level of experience to match the complexity of the case, previous involvement in similar cases and even personality – does the case require a forthright or a subtle approach; passion or a cool head?

You should have a say in choosing the person to present the case in court – after all, it concerns the child, your client. You need to have complete confidence in your advocate. If you do not know the advocate suggested, ask your lawyer why she thinks he is the right choice, and look him up on the internet. Ask your colleagues if they have come across him before. Local authorities should be proactive in sharing information. Every time a social worker goes to court and sees an advocate in action – no matter which party he represents – she should make a note of her impressions and share it with colleagues.

---

1   *Re R (Care: disclosure: nature of proceedings)* [2002] 1FLR 755, High Court Family
     Division.

There is nothing better than ensuring that someone who gave you a good run for your money in one case is on your side next time! Equally, if an advocate is not impressive, you do not want to entrust your next case to him.

If a barrister or other advocate is to be used for the final hearing, he should be instructed early on and you should have a single consistent representative for the whole case. Short of a genuine emergency, there is no excuse for last-minute instructions. If you are the key worker in a case, you should have a meeting with the barrister – known as a 'conference with counsel' – well before any contested hearing. This gives you a chance to discuss the case in detail and to get to know each other before the big day.

Build in time for proper feedback and reflection with your legal team at the end of the case, whatever the outcome. Too often the response when the hearing is over is to breathe a sigh of relief and rush on to the next case, so we fail to learn lessons and are forced to re-invent the wheel or repeat mistakes time and again. Every case should teach us something, and that learning needs to be shared with the whole department – otherwise one team could learn an important lesson only to have someone from another team repeat the same mistake, possibly in front of the same judge, the following week. Neither should we assume that we can only learn from mistakes. When cases go well, we should also allow time to analyse what worked and try to share and repeat the experience.

QUESTIONS FOR REFLECTION

- What can you do to make your relationship with your lawyers work?

- Could any inter-departmental procedures be introduced to improve teamwork with lawyers?

The parents

You are a professional, working as part of a team and supported by colleagues from your own and partner agencies. For you, the case is part of the job you have chosen to do. The case is not about you; it is not personal. For the parents, it is a different story – nothing could be more personal; their life histories are examined, the most intimate aspects of their lives dissected and, at the end of it all, they may lose their children. For a moment put aside your professional conviction that what you are doing is the right thing for the child and put yourself in the parents' position. How would you feel in their shoes? How would you behave? Of course, circumstances of care cases vary widely and parents come from differing backgrounds with a range of difficulties, but almost invariably they love their children and believe that they are in the right, that you are wrong and your action is unjustified. This dictates their response to proceedings. Remembering this will help you to keep a cool head when you are faced with a response you think is unreasonable, unfair or even aggressive.

Use your knowledge of the particular parents in your case to anticipate how they are likely to react and what they are likely to say and do. Discuss these anticipated responses with your legal team and prepare in advance how to deal with them.

Disadvantaged parents

Sometimes a parent involved in proceedings is incapable of understanding the proceedings and giving instructions to a solicitor because of a profound learning disability or severe mental health problems. In those circumstances, the parent's interests may be represented by the Official Solicitor (commonly known as 'the OS'), a central government appointee with an office staffed by civil servants. Only the court can invite the OS to act, and he requires medical or psychiatric confirmation of the parent's condition before consenting to take on the case. The OS then appoints a solicitor, gives instructions on the parent's behalf and files a report in the proceedings. The role is strictly limited to representing adults while they are incapacitated; so if, for example, the mother's mental health improves during the proceedings, the OS withdraws and the mother can instruct her own solicitor. If you are aware that an adult involved in proceedings may need the help of the OS, raise this point as soon as possible as it should be dealt with at the earliest stage in proceedings, to avoid causing delay and/or injustice.

The parent's legal representative

All parents in care proceedings are entitled to have competent representation from a lawyer who specialises in care proceedings, and they receive free Legal Aid for this. Although you might be tempted to think that your life might be easier if the parents were not well represented, in fact cases go much more smoothly if everyone involved is competent. As a matter of principle, no one should have a child removed without having their case properly argued and the child himself needs to know that his parents were fairly treated by the system.

The parent's solicitor has a challenging job on strictly limited Legal Aid funding. She has to go through the evidence in detail with her clients, ensuring they understand it and noting their responses. Where clients have learning difficulties, substance abuse issues, mental health or personality problems, cannot read or are simply and understandably emotional, this is a lengthy and delicate task. Just because the solicitor is 'on their side' does not mean that she is immune from parents' sometimes angry or emotional responses. Parents' solicitors can be on the receiving end of verbal abuse, insults or threats from difficult or distressed clients. Except in cases extreme enough to justify the solicitor refusing to continue to act, this is all part of the job, and the solicitor should not let anyone else know that the working relationship is anything other than harmonious.

The solicitor's job is to advise her client on the law and the strength of the evidence, on the response to the allegations, legal procedures, strategies and tactics. Sometimes this includes telling the parents that the local authority's case is so strong that, no matter what, they are likely to lose their children. The parents may accept that, and the strategy then turns to damage limitation, such as accepting a care order, but seeking more contact or resisting adoption. On the other hand they may insist on fighting the case come what may. If so, the solicitor must follow her instructions and find a way of putting up a convincing fight, however futile she knows it to be. You will never know that, in private, the solicitor has told her clients their case is hopeless. Do not assume that a lawyer always actually believes in the case she is presenting, however passionately she appears to do so!

Sometimes a parent has to fight on two fronts. For example, two parents may each blame the other for injuries to the child. For each, the objective is two-fold – first, to defeat the local authority's criticisms and second, to lay the blame on the other parent.

QUESTION FOR REFLECTION

- What can you do to ensure that the parents' right to a fair trial is respected while still putting the child's welfare first?

The child's representatives

The child is always a party to care proceedings[2] and is represented by both a Children's Guardian and a solicitor. The role of Children's Guardian was introduced after the scandal of Maria Colwell's death in 1973. Seven-year-old Maria was returned home from the safety of foster care when the court sanctioned the plan agreed between the local authority and the mother. Maria was then killed by her stepfather. The enquiry into her death highlighted the need for an independent voice for the child in proceedings and the Children Act 1975 created the role of Guardian (then called Guardian *ad Litem*) to represent the child's interests in the case. Guardians are automatically appointed as soon as care proceedings are issued. The Children and Family Court Advisory and Support Service[3] (universally known as CAFCASS) nominates the Guardian for the particular case.

Like any other party, the child is also entitled to legal representation. The Guardian appoints as solicitor for the child a member of the Law Society's Children Law Accreditation Scheme[4], who must do the work on the case personally wherever possible.

How the solicitor and Guardian work together depends on whether the child is competent and this is a question for the solicitor concerned. Age is one factor; the older the child, the more likely he is to be competent. The issue is certainly considered for any child of secondary school age. Another factor is the child's level of understanding as learning difficulties or emotional problems can impede his competence to instruct.

If the child cannot give his own instructions to the solicitor (because he is too young or for some other reason such as cognitive impairment),

---

2   Children may be made parties to private law proceedings (such as disputes about residence or contact) but this is not automatic.

3   CAFCASS is part of the Ministry of Justice in England, and CAFCASS Cymru is under the Welsh Government.

4   For more information on this scheme or to find children law specialists in your area, visit the website www.lawsociety.org.uk/accreditation/specialist-schemes/children-law/, accessed on 24 November 2014.

the solicitor and Guardian work together. The Guardian effectively acts as the client, giving instructions to the solicitor, who in turn advises the Guardian on law, evidence, procedure, strategy and tactics. The working relationship should be robust, mutually respectful but challenging and, as with all solicitor/client relationships, discussions between the two are confidential.

But if the child is competent to do so, he gives his own instructions to the solicitor. What if the child's wishes conflict with the Guardian's views of his best interests? In this case, the solicitor follows the child's instructions and the Guardian has to fend for herself, so that both cases are put to the court. However, although the child is the solicitor's client, he is unlikely to file a formal statement, attend court or give evidence.

The child's team's job is to put forward an independent view of the child's best interests and to ensure that his wishes and feelings are made clear to the court. No doubt you feel that, as the child's social worker, you are already doing this – after all, the child is your client too and you are only taking action because you and your department believe it to be the best thing for the child. You may also feel that you know the child and his wishes and feelings better than the Guardian, and you may be right – if so, you can make this point to the court in due course. But the fact is that your authority has, by taking the proceedings in the first place, already nailed its colours to the mast and is inevitably in a partisan position at the very outset of the case. The Guardian and the child's solicitor come in afresh and look at the case with new eyes, testing, challenging and double checking. Guardians are now obliged to file their case analysis at an early stage in the case.

It is important to remember that a Guardian is not a duplicate social worker – she does not work the case, nor is she your supervisor – it is not her role to advise you on how to prepare your case or to help you through your difficulties, and she should always scrupulously retain her independence.

Like everyone else, Guardians have budget and time constraints and the work they devote to a case is necessarily limited. Research published in 2013[5] indicated that Guardians had contact with the child in almost all cases (the exceptions being those involving very

---

5   The Work of Children's Guardians in Care Cases published by CAFCASS, available at www.cafcass.gov.uk/media/187312/the_work_of_children_s_guardians_in_care_cases.pdf, accessed on 26 November 2014.

young children) with an average of three contacts per case with the child, including face-to-face meetings in a third of cases, including all cases involving children over 12. Most of their work is done in the early stages of the proceedings.

Always treat the Guardian with respect (the court certainly will), listen to her views and take her comments into account – but do not feel obliged to agree with her or follow her bidding. However authoritative she may be, the court, not the Guardian, makes the decision and it is not bound to follow her recommendation. Indeed, Macur LJ[6] referred to:

> the continuing misconception that the evidence and opinion of a Children's Guardian, however demonstrably poorly rooted or reasoned, carries additional weight by virtue of their 'special' status. It must be firmly squashed. The Children's Guardian is required to proffer advice to the court but in doing so becomes a witness subject to the same judicial scrutiny as any other. A Children's Guardian starts with no special advantage.

If, after proper consideration, you and your department disagree with the Guardian, stick to your guns, and be prepared to justify your position and explain your reasoning. Guardians are social workers by training, and their qualifications are the same as yours. As with any profession, some are better than others. Many are excellent but some are not. You may feel that the Guardian has not spent enough time with the child, or has not approached a case with sufficient diligence, objectivity or competence. Children deserve better than that and the local authority should be willing to challenge inadequate work by a Guardian (you can be sure a Guardian will have no hesitation in pointing out any inadequacies on the local authority's part). Your advocate should be instructed, for example, to suggest to the court that your view of the child, formed over a long period of consistent work, should be preferred to that of a Guardian who has hardly seen the child.

Under s42 Children Act 1989, the Guardian is entitled to examine and take copies of any Social Services records relating to the proceedings or to the child. She can then include those documents or refer to them in her report or her evidence in court. As a matter of courtesy, she should tell you which documents she is copying and

---

6   *MW and Hertfordshire County Council v A and Others* [2014] EWCA Civ 405.

what she is proposing to use. She is not entitled to see your legal advice or any correspondence or notes of discussions between you and your lawyers, which are covered by legal professional privilege. If you are in any doubt about what documents the Guardian should see, consult your lawyers. Guardians should, like social workers, also be prepared to produce their notes of relevant conversations and incidents. Feel free, therefore, to ask the Guardian to provide a copy of her notes, for example, of an important interview with the child.

QUESTIONS FOR REFLECTION

- What is your attitude towards Guardians in general? How does this affect your working relationships with them?

- How can you achieve the right balance of co-operation and independence when working with Guardians?

The court

The Family Court is now a single entity with a unified administration. It generally sits in the Magistrates' or County Court with at least one Designated Family Centre in each area. There are different levels of judges within the Family Court, ranging from lay judges (magistrates) to High Court Judges.

The court is entrusted with the job of deciding the case. This sounds obvious, but think for a moment about what it actually entails. How would you like to have to decide whether a child should be permanently separated from his parents? Imagine the burden of that responsibility. In that position, what would you want from the parties? When you are preparing and giving your evidence, think how it would feel to be in the court's shoes and provide information to help the judge perform this difficult task.

Judges are qualified and experienced lawyers, trained to analyse facts against a legal framework. Magistrates, on the other hand, have no legal qualifications and sit part-time alongside their other occupations. Their strengths lie in common sense and life experience. They are guided by a legally qualified Justices' Clerk.

When you picture a judge in your mind's eye, do you see a man or a woman? Is this person young? Black? Disabled? Openly gay? The fact is that, although things are changing, most judges are still white and male, especially in the higher echelons of the judiciary. In 2004, Lady Hale became the first woman to be appointed to the House of Lords. Unfortunately, at the time of writing she remains the lone female voice in the Supreme Court. There are no black or ethnic minority judges in the Supreme Court or Court of Appeal. In the High Court the position is a little better, with approximately 5 per cent non-white judges. The slow pace of change is perhaps inevitable as eligibility to apply for judicial appointment depends on specific periods already spent as qualified lawyers and then it takes time to climb the judicial ladder. This means that today's judges reflect the composition of entrants to the legal profession (particularly the bar as most judges are former barristers rather than solicitors) 10, 20 or even 30 years ago, when most lawyers came from a narrow social group. The position should improve with time.

Magistrates, in contrast, are far more diverse and socially representative. The previous 'twin-set and pearls' image is now outdated thanks to a positive effort to appoint magistrates from varied backgrounds, ethnic groups, social classes and age groups. The minimum age to be a magistrate is 18, and in 2006 a 19-year-old woman became the youngest person to be appointed to date; but the majority of magistrates are still over 40. Approximately 8 per cent of magistrates come from ethnic minorities. A specific effort was also made to encourage applications from people with disabilities. Magistrates are therefore more socially representative of their community and, as it is a part-time post, also represent a wide range of professions and life experience. On the other hand, they do not necessarily have the academic background or intellectual ability of judges, although they undergo a carefully designed programme of training.

QUESTION FOR REFLECTION

- How might the composition of the court affect the way you present your evidence?

FREQUENTLY ASKED QUESTIONS

What's the difference between a lawyer, advocate,
counsel, solicitor and barrister?

'Lawyer' is a generic term for all legal professionals including solicitors, barristers, legal executives and academics. 'Advocate' is the term for the person who presents the case in court, whichever branch of the legal profession they belong to. 'Counsel' is another name for a barrister. 'Solicitors' and 'barristers' form the two main branches of the legal profession. Their training separates after the degree stage, both then undertaking a combination of further study and practical training. Solicitors work directly with their clients, whereas barristers are generally briefed by solicitors, who still send papers tied up with red tape. Solicitors deal with correspondence and negotiations and also have the right of audience in some courts including the Family Court, but they cannot appear in the Crown Court, which is reserved for barristers, who have the right of audience in all courts. Barristers often specialise in advocacy and also give written opinions on complex points of law.

What is a QC and when would one be involved in a case?

QC stands for Queen's Counsel, also often known as a 'silk' (the fabric of their gowns). Only senior members of the profession are eligible to be appointed as QCs and the vast majority are barristers. They are only involved in exceptionally complicated cases and often are not instructed until the case reaches the appeal courts.

What is the Law Society's Children Law Accreditation Scheme?

This consists of specialist solicitors who have attended a training course, demonstrated technical knowledge of family law and practical experience of care cases, attended an interview and provided references. Children's law is a very specialist topic and it is important that parties are represented by someone with particular knowledge and expertise.

How can a lawyer represent a paedophile,
or someone he knows is guilty?

Dr Johnson summed this up perfectly in the eighteenth century:

a lawyer has no business with the justice or injustice of the cause which he undertakes, unless the client asks his opinion and then he is bound to give it honestly. The justice or injustice of the cause is to be decided by the judge.

Quite simply the lawyer's job is to be the client's specialist mouthpiece, and every client is entitled to be represented to the best of the lawyer's ability. The lawyer's private view of the case or his client is entirely irrelevant.

Do parties in care proceedings always get Legal Aid?

At the time of writing, in care proceedings, parents and children automatically have the right to receive Legal Aid, regardless of their means or the merits of their case. However, the Legal Aid system is under strain, lawyers are increasingly reluctant to undertake Legal Aid work due to poor remuneration and excessive bureaucracy, and there are constant proposals for reform.

What qualifications do Children's Guardians have?

CAFCASS requires a minimum of a Diploma in Social Work and three years' post-qualification experience in social work practice with children and families at risk.

What is meant by HHJ, J and LJ?

These are abbreviations for judges' titles. HHJ Brown refers to a County Court Judge, His or Her Honour Judge Brown. A High Court Judge is Mr or Mrs Justice Brown, shortened to Brown J. LJ after the judge's name shows that he or she has reached the Court of Appeal, and stands for Lord or Lady Justice.

How do lawyers find reports of decided cases?

There are official law reports for decided cases, such as the All England Law Reports and Weekly Law Reports. There are also specialist reports, the most important of which, for our purposes, is the Family Law Reports. Judgments are also published on the internet.

The name of the case in children's matters gives only an initial, rather than a name, to preserve confidentiality, and further details in brackets sometimes give an indication of the case content.

The case reference indicates the year of the case in square brackets, followed by the level of court which decided the case: EWHC (Fam) means the Family Division of the High Court, EWCA (Civ) means the Civil Division of the Court of Appeal and UKSC refers to the Supreme Court of the United Kingdom. So *Re B (A Child)* [2013] UKSC 33 was the 33rd case heard by the Supreme Court in 2013.

QUESTION FOR REFLECTION

- How can understanding the respective roles and responsibilities of the participants in the case help you to perform your own role better?

Chapter 4

Evidence

The idea of evidence

Both parties want to win the case. To persuade the court, each party puts his case to court by a combination of evidence (giving his version of events while undermining the other party's version) and argument (asking the court to interpret the evidence in his favour). Academic lawyers write volumes and practising lawyers argue for hours about the law of evidence. This chapter, therefore, can only give an essential outline. Fortunately for social workers, the rules of evidence in care proceedings are more relaxed than in almost any other kind of case.

Put at its most basic, evidence is the information which a court can take into account in making its decision. Rules of 'admissibility of evidence' determine what information the court is allowed to hear; if information is inadmissible, the court cannot even consider it, however relevant or convincing it might seem to be, however much the court might wish to hear it or justice might seem to demand it.

If evidence is admissible, the court can take it into account. It is then up to the court to decide how much weight to give it – that is, to decide how plausible or persuasive it is. It is important, therefore, not to confuse admissibility with weight – just because something is admissible does not mean that it is convincing, or adds anything to the case. Not all admissible evidence is worth presenting to the court.

Think of the classic image of the scales of justice – two scale pans suspended in balance. Each party puts his evidence onto his side of the scales to try to make them tip his way. Only admissible evidence can be put into the scales, but the mere fact that something is allowed does not mean it will have any effect – you can put a feather onto the scales, but it will not make the scales move.

Burden of proof

The concept of the 'burden of proof ' essentially determines whose job it is to make the scales move his way, and the general principle of English law is that it is up to the party bringing the case to prove it. So, in a criminal case, the prosecution must prove that the defendant committed the crime; it is not up to the defendant to show that he is innocent. In care proceedings, it is the local authority's job to prove that the threshold criteria are met and the child's welfare demands the making of an order; the parents do not have to prove that they are 'good enough'.

In court, the applicant (the prosecution in a criminal trial, the local authority in care proceedings) presents its case first and attempts to prove it by putting its evidence into the scales, making them move in its favour. The defendant/respondent cross-examines the applicant's witnesses to undermine the impact of the evidence, so that although the information may still be in the final reckoning, its weight is reduced.

That defendant/respondent in turn produces his own case, to undermine or neutralise the applicant's evidence – effectively to remove weight from the applicant's side of the scales – and to put evidence into his own scale pan to tip the balance in his favour.

Standard of proof

The next question is how far the scales have to move to allow the applicant to 'win'. This is the essential concept of the 'standard of proof', discussed in Chapter 2. In a criminal case, to achieve proof beyond reasonable doubt, the prosecution has to tip the scales much further than the applicant in a civil matter.

In family cases, the standard of proof is the 'balance of probabilities'. In the past, case law indicated that the interpretation of the standard could vary according to the seriousness of the allegations (the more serious the allegation, the greater the evidence required). Now, it is clear that this is not the case – as Baroness Hale said,[1] 'the standard of proof…is the simple balance of probabilities, neither more nor less'. So the local authority must satisfy the court that its case is more likely than not to be correct.

Although this is a significantly lower test than that faced by the Crown Prosecution Service, it is very important not to be complacent

---

1   *B (Children)* [2008] UKHL 35 para. 70.

and think that the civil standard is an easy hurdle to overcome. It is not enough to show grounds for suspicion or concern; the court must be 'satisfied' that the case is made out. This is a fundamental principle of the Children Act, as Lady Hale explained:[2]

> The threshold is there to protect both the children and their parents from unjustified intervention in their lives. It would provide no protection at all if it could be established on the basis of unsubstantiated suspicions.

Your case must be based on evidence. As Black LJ said,[3] there must be 'active thought from the outset about what the factual and evidential basis of a local authority's case is'. As she went on to say,[4] if the parents dispute the case, remember that 'allegations which are denied are not facts. If the local authority need to rely upon them as part of their case, they will have to produce the evidence to establish them'. Your recommendations depend on the evidence: 'The assessment and opinions of social workers and those of other professionals will only hold water if the facts upon which they proceed are properly identified and turn out actually to be facts.'[5]

Suspicions and gut feelings are not facts, but if you think it through, there may be evidence underlying those feelings. If you analyse it, there is a reason behind your instinctive reactions – why do you feel as you do? 'He gives me the creeps' is not evidence; 'He frequently turns the conversation to sexual topics' or 'He avoids eye contact whenever the subject of sexual abuse is raised' are factual observations and might well be evidence when seen in context. In her Final Report,[6] Professor Eileen Munro referred to neuropsychological research into intuitive and emotional responses:

> Intuition is sometimes presented as a mysterious or mystical process, but its physical location in the brain and the features of the process are understood. It is only mysterious in the sense that it is generally an unconscious process that occurs automatically in response to

---

2   *B (Children)* at para. 54.
3   *P (A Child)* [2013] EWCA Civ 963 para. 111.
4   *Re P* at para. 115.
5   *Black LJ in Re P* at para. 112.
6   Para. 6.25 *The Munro Review of Child Protection: Final Report. A Child Centred System.* Professor Eileen Munro, DfE 2011, www.gov.uk/government/publications/munro-review-of-child-protection-final-report-a-child-centred-system, accessed on 24 November 2014.

perceptions, integrating a wide range of data to produce a judgment in a relatively effortless way. It is very rapid and relatively independent of language, oriented towards identifying patterns. It need not remain unconscious but can be articulated and this ability can be improved with guided practice and with explicit attention to eliciting the evidence that the unconscious was noting and interpreting.

Do not feel you must dismiss your intuition in the court process, but be very careful to present the evidence upon which it was based.

Neither should you dismiss pieces of information which may seem minor. As Lord Nicholls said,[7] 'the range of facts which may be taken into account is infinite…and facts which are minor or even trivial if considered in isolation, when taken together may suffice to satisfy the court of the likelihood of future harm'.

Evidence in care proceedings is like a jigsaw: each piece on its own may make no sense at all – it is only when all the pieces are put together that the picture emerges. When you are building a case you need to make sure that you give the court all the pieces of the jigsaw.

Types of evidence

Factual evidence

Clearly, the most fundamental form of evidence is plain factual information which tells the court 'this is what happened', 'this is what I did' or 'this is what I saw'. It comes from eye witnesses, and people directly involved in events. Whether the person is telling the truth or not is a matter for the court to judge and courts are well used to deciding between contradictory versions of events.

Real and documentary evidence

The court is not limited to considering words; objects can be evidence, the classic example being exhibiting the alleged murder weapon in a Criminal Court. This is less common in family cases, but occasionally objects are produced, such as the belt used to hit a child. Do not overlook the possibility of producing relevant objects in an appropriate case – they can be very powerful.

Documents, including photographs, can also be relevant and very effective evidence. Police photos or video recordings of a drugs

---

7   Re H & R (Child Sexual Abuse: Standard of Proof) [1996] 1FLR 80 at p.101 B–C.

raid, for example, can be influential, showing exactly what home conditions were like. Photographs of a child's injuries can be vitally important, remembering of course that injuries such as bruises must be photographed quickly before they fade. In one case where the child had almost died from malnutrition, photographs taken on his admission to hospital were produced alongside photographs taken after three months in foster care. He was transformed from a bag of bones to a normal healthy-looking child. Those pictures were worth a thousand words.

Diagrams or graphs can also be valuable evidence. In care proceedings, centile charts are often produced by health professionals, and these can be graphic in both senses. One chart showed a child's growth as flat, falling further and further away from the original centile, until a particular date when it suddenly shot up steeply, recording remarkable catch-up growth. The rest of the evidence demonstrated that the dramatic change coincided with the time the father left home. In other cases, you may find a similar change after reception into foster care. A simple line on a chart can speak volumes.

A body map can illustrate the size and distribution of injuries and give a more striking impression of the extent of injuries than a long paragraph of description.

Video recordings can also be produced in evidence and are especially important for interviews with children. If these are conducted following the 'Achieving Best Evidence'[8] guidelines, they can be produced in both criminal and care cases. Interviewing children is a skilled task, and should only be undertaken by specially trained and experienced staff. Properly done, video interviews can be powerful. They have the advantage of recording not only the child's responses, but also the questions asked, so the court and parties can clearly see whether the child has in any way been led by the questioner. As well as hearing the child's words, viewers can see his body language. In one interview a five-year-old who was bright and cheery during the 'rapport' phase of the interview physically crumpled as soon as the subject of sexual abuse was raised. There was no substitute for seeing

---

8   *Achieving Best Evidence in Criminal Proceedings: Guidance on interviewing victims and witnesses, and guidance on using special measures.* Ministry of Justice 2011. www.justice.gov.uk/downloads/victims-and-witnesses/vulnerable-witnesses/achieving-best-evidence-criminal-proceedings.pdf, accessed on 25 August 2014.

the video – paragraphs of description would never have conveyed what the viewers saw.

In another case the interview transcript showed that the child said, 'Daddy hurt my bottom,' and those who believed that he had been sexually abused could easily have leapt to the conclusion that this was a disclosure. In fact, the video revealed that, as he said these words, the child clearly gestured with his hand in a smacking motion – he was telling us that his father spanked him.

Whenever real or photographic evidence is produced, it must be authenticated, for example, by the person who took the photograph, confirming that this is indeed the photograph he took, when, where and how it was done and confirming that it accurately records what he saw. This is even more important in these days of easy manipulation of digital images.

As for any other kind of evidence, advance disclosure to all parties is required. Other parties must be sent copies of such evidence in advance, as well as transcripts of audio or video recordings.

QUESTION FOR REFLECTION

- How can you be sure rigorously to evidence the facts on which your case depends?

- What information other than written evidence can you use to establish your case?

Hearsay evidence

Put simply, hearsay evidence is anything which is not from the witness's own direct experience. The starting point of English law has always been that hearsay is inadmissible, for the simple reason that it is generally of no use to the court. Imagine a witness telling a criminal court that he heard that the defendant had robbed the bank. What use would that be? All the witness could confirm was that he heard it, and give details about who told him, where, when, how – but he could not tell the court one way or the other whether it was true. He would waste the court's time.

Hearsay does not just refer to information heard, but really anything other than evidence from the witness's own direct experience. This includes reports from other professionals ('The health visitor told me the home was unhygienic'), or information from the file prior to your involvement ('My predecessor discussed hygiene with Mrs Smith').

What children tell you is hearsay evidence – in your evidence, you can confirm to the court that it is indeed what the child said, but you cannot say one way of the other whether it is actually true. In our sexual abuse scenario in Chapter 2, Amy's allegations of sexual abuse against her stepfather Barry are recorded in a video interview. At Barry's criminal trial, the video is shown to the Crown Court, but it cannot stand alone; someone has to be cross-examined to test out the truth of the evidence. The interviewers cannot give evidence for Amy – that would be hearsay and so not admissible in a criminal trial. The only person who can give Amy's evidence in the Criminal Court is Amy herself. Thanks to the provisions of the Youth Justice and Criminal Evidence Act 1999, some concessions are made to Amy – for example, she gives evidence by live TV link rather than in the courtroom itself, and the barristers and judge remove their wigs and gowns, but the fact remains that Amy herself has to go to court to answer questions to test out the truth or otherwise of her evidence.

Amy is also subject to care proceedings and here the position is different. Because of an important exception for children's cases,[9] hearsay is admissible, so this time Amy does not have to go to court. Her video is shown to the court, and the interviewers can give evidence about what she said. The hearsay evidence itself is admissible. This exception does not just apply to formal interviews: foster carers, teachers and social workers can tell the court what the child said and the court can take this information fully into account.

Children attending the Family Court

What role do children themselves play in the court process? The Court of Appeal has said:[10]

> 'Our collective understanding of these matters and how best to 'hear' a young person within the court setting, is developing and is still, to an extent, in its infancy.'

It is anticipated that early in 2015, new court rules will be introduced to ensure that, at an early stage in every case, consideration is given

---

9   Children (Admissibility of Hearsay Evidence) Order 1993 SI 1993/621.

10   Re KP (A Child) [2014] EWCA 554 at para 52).

to the child's participation. In appropriate cases, this can include the child meeting the judge to help her understand the proceedings better and reassure her that the judge has heard her wishes and feelings. Of course such meetings must be handled carefully. Until the new rules are introduced, guidelines issued by the Family Justice Council should be followed.[11]

Can a child actually give evidence in care proceedings? Previously there was thought to be a presumption against this, but this is no longer so.[12] Instead, the respective parties' human rights must be balanced, especially the right to a fair trial as against the child's welfare. However it is clear that it remains very unusual for a child to give evidence in care proceedings and she is highly unlikely to be forced to do so if unwilling.

If a child does give evidence, careful consideration must be given to how this is to be managed and all necessary steps must be taken to ensure that her welfare is protected including, for example, giving evidence by video link, or answering only questions posed by the judge, not the advocates. New court rules supported by a training programme are expected in early 2015; in the meantime guidelines issued by The Family Justice Council should be followed.[13]

You should consider the child's participation in the court case at an early stage and discuss it with your legal team. Be prepared to make or oppose any necessary applications before the court.

Hearsay evidence from adult witnesses

The hearsay exception is not limited to evidence from children themselves, but can apply to information from anyone in a children's case. Should adults who make allegations have the same protection as children? In one case, a couple applied to look after their granddaughter who needed a home. Sixteen years earlier, they had fostered a girl, now adult, who for the first time alleged that the grandfather had sexually abused her when she was in the couple's care. The social

---

11 *Guidelines for Judges Meeting Children who are subject to Family Proceedings*, available at www.fnf.org.uk/downloads/Guidelines_for_Judges_Meeting_Children.pdf, accessed on 25 August 2014.

12 *W (Children)* [2010] UKSC 12 (Supreme Court).

13 Working Party of the Family Justice Council: *Guidelines in relation to children giving evidence in family proceedings*, issued December 2011, available at www.judiciary.gov.uk/ JCO%2FDocuments%2FFJC%2FFJC_Guidelines_+in_relation_children_+giving_ evidence_+in_+family_+proceedings_Dec2011.pdf, accessed on 25 August 2014.

worker interviewed the woman, believed her and reported on her interview in evidence to the court. The magistrates made a finding that the allegation was true, on the basis of the social worker's hearsay evidence. The grandparents appealed and won – the magistrates had no right to accept evidence in that form or to make a finding. The President of the Family Division of the High Court declared her dismay at the 'sloppy half-hearted…sympathetic interview without any sort of rigour of questioning…to have that accepted by the court as evidence that brands a man as a sexual abuser is entirely unacceptable'.[14]

Essentially, children may generally be protected from coming to the Family Court, but adults are expected to stand up for themselves.

Notice the consequences of the inadequate work in this case. If the grandfather was innocent, he and his family suffered the stress of false allegations and the child's placement was delayed. If the allegations were true, the inadequacy of the case presentation placed the granddaughter at risk.

Hearsay in social work statements

Sometimes social workers' statements seem to be nothing but hearsay, reporting information from the police, health visitor, teacher and social work assistant. It may be admissible, but is it helpful to the court? Is it the best way of presenting the information?

Hearsay or direct evidence?

Mrs Goff, health visitor, makes a referral to Ms Hutchinson, social worker, about baby Ian. There are two ways of giving this information to court:

1. Ms Hutchinson can record in her statement: 'Mrs Goff, the health visitor, telephoned me to report her concerns that Ian was being handled roughly by his mother.' This gives the court the basic facts, but what can be tested about this statement? Ms Hutchinson can be asked whether the conversation really

---

14 *Dame Elizabeth Butler-Sloss, 5 Re D (Sexual abuse allegations: evidence of adult victim)* [2002] 1FLR 723, High Court Family Division, p.728 D.

happened, and the exact words Mrs Goff used, but she is limited to reporting the conversation itself. The answers to any further questions – exactly what Mrs Goff saw, why she was concerned, what she did about it, how experienced she is, her professional opinion about the appropriateness of the handling – must be 'I'm sorry, you'd have to ask Mrs Goff about that'.

2. Mrs Goff can make her own statement to the court and, if required, attend to give oral evidence. She can set out her qualifications and experience and describe exactly what she saw, her professional opinion and what she did about it. Her evidence can be tested out by cross examination, giving the mother the chance to challenge the truth of the allegations or Mrs Goff's interpretation of what she saw, and giving the court the opportunity to form a view about Mrs Goff's reliability and professionalism. Her first-hand evidence is bound to be more vivid and detailed than anything Ms Hutchinson could report. Ms Hutchinson can refer to Mrs Goff's evidence briefly in her own statement when she pulls together all the concerns for Ian.

If you were the judge, which would you prefer?

The general principle is that the court is always entitled to the best evidence available – that is, direct personal evidence wherever possible. You owe it to the court and to the child to present the case as strongly as possible.

Whenever you are preparing a case, consider who should give evidence about each point you need to prove. Your lawyer does not know who is involved in a child's life unless you tell him, and so he does not know who to approach for evidence without your assistance. As part of your case preparation you and your legal team need to consider who can provide all the pieces of the jigsaw. If hearsay is unavoidable, explain the reason why direct evidence is not available, for example, that the original social worker has emigrated to Australia, or that the lay informant asked to remain anonymous.

Remember, too, that just because you are the key worker representing your department, that does not mean that you have to give every piece of social work evidence yourself. For example, if your care plan for the child is adoption, the court needs evidence about how realistic the plan is and how quickly adopters can be found. If you are not an adoption specialist, you are unlikely to have the relevant information or experience, so a member of the adoption team needs to give that evidence. Similarly, if a decision in the case was made by a senior member of your department, then only she can explain why that decision was reached and she needs to be prepared to come to court. If another worker tries to explain a decision which was not hers, she is giving the court second-hand evidence and that is not good enough.

Nor can you answer for other agencies or departments within your authority. For example, if a child has received inadequate educational provision, it is for an education representative, not you, to explain it. Sometimes just a letter from the legal department requesting evidence or court attendance works wonders in securing services.

If the authority is likely to be criticised, or there is an issue about broader policy, it is wrong for a career grade social worker to take the flak and you should not accept it – a senior member of the department should attend. On more than one occasion the courts have expressed fury towards local authorities which failed to produce a senior member of the department to answer to their actions. In one case the authority had failed to produce a pathway plan for a child with severe disabilities despite a legal obligation and a court order to do so, a failure Wall LJ described as 'lamentable, totally lamentable' and 'worthy of the highest condemnation'. Attending court to explain the authority's position was not a senior manager but, as Wall LJ put it, 'some wretched social worker…put forward as a sacrificial lamb, as a victim to this court's anger and legitimate wrath'. There is no reason why any career grade social worker should be put in that position and senior managers should take the responsibility which is rightfully theirs. Why no one sought a witness summons to require a senior officer to come to court is a mystery. In that case, the order made was endorsed with a penal notice which meant that, in the event of default, the Director of Children's Services (not the social worker) could have ended up in prison.

Opinion evidence

What is an opinion? Sometimes it is explicit – for example, 'In my professional opinion she is suffering from postnatal depression'. However, consider sentences like 'John shows disturbed behaviour' or

'Mr Kent was drunk when he came to the meeting'. These are expressed as if they are facts, but what is or is not 'disturbed' is a value judgment – an opinion – and it is doubtful that you performed a breathalyser test on Mr Kent to establish his alcohol consumption; your observations of his behaviour and demeanour led you to the opinion that he was drunk. Be clear in your own mind whether you are actually reporting facts or expressing an opinion.

The starting point of English law is that opinion evidence is generally inadmissible, because most of the time it is useless. Any witness could express a view about whether or not the child should go home, but how would that help the court? In most cases, it is simply a waste of the court's time, and anyway, deciding whether the child goes home is the court's job. The only time a witness's opinion is worth considering is when it is based on expertise which the court itself does not have. For that reason, there is an exception to the general rule, allowing experts to give opinion evidence if, but only if, it is relevant and necessary.

Experts

Who, then, is an expert? How can expertise be established? A person can only be instructed to act as an expert witness in a case if the court makes specific directions. (For more information on instructing experts in care proceedings *see* Chapter 8.) Other witnesses (for example, those who already work with the family) may be able to give opinion evidence if the court accepts them as experts in a particular field. Ultimately it is for the court to decide whether a particular witness is an expert and, if there is a dispute, there can be a mini trial within a trial for the court to determine the issue. Expertise can be established by formal qualifications and training but also by experience. For example, a foster mother without a piece of paper to her name but who has fostered 50 pre-adopt babies has expertise and can assist the court with her opinions on the care and behaviour of young babies. Conversely, a witness who happens to have a psychology degree acquired ten years ago, but who has never practised in the field will not be permitted to give opinion evidence on psychological issues.

Social workers as experts

In recent years, social workers have at times seemed almost to conspire in the de-skilling of their own profession. But it is clear that we are at a crossroads and the social work profession has an opportunity to step forward and claim its rightful place. As Sir James Munby P explained in his 'View from the President's Chambers'[15]:

> Social workers are experts... In every care case we have at least two experts – a social worker and a guardian – yet we have grown up with a culture of believing that they are not really experts and that we therefore need experts with a capital E. The plain fact is that much of the time we do not.

> Social workers may not be experts for the purposes of Family Procedure Rules Part 25, but that does not mean that they are not experts in every other sense of the word. They are, and we must recognise them and treat them as such.

> One of the problems is that in recent years too many social workers have come to feel undervalued, disempowered and de-skilled. In part at least this is an unhappy consequence of the way in which care proceedings have come to be dealt with by the courts. If the revised Public Law Outline is properly implemented one of its outcomes will, I hope, be to re-position social workers as trusted professionals playing the central role in care proceedings which too often of late has been overshadowed by our unnecessary use of and reliance upon other experts.

This welcome endorsement of the professionalism of social workers is timely and important. Claim your expertise. You have qualifications and experience (which may include relevant previous professional experience or even activities in a private capacity, such as being a youth leader). Take time to consider what you know and what expertise you have to assist the court. If you are challenged in court on what right you have to reach a particular recommendation, you need to know how to justify your status as an expert – you will hardly enhance your credibility if you cannot answer!

It is equally important to know where your boundaries lie, and where are the limits of your expertise. One of the problems of social

---

15 'The View from the President's Chambers (2) – The process of reform: the revised PLO and the local authority', [2013], pp.6–7, available at www.judiciary.gov.uk/publications/view-from-presidents-chambers/, accessed on 3 September, 2014.

work is that it is a broad subject; for example, you know about child development, but not as much as a paediatrician; you know about family functioning, but perhaps not as much as a psychologist. Be very careful never to get drawn in beyond the limits of your knowledge or seem to be claiming expertise you do not have, or you will find yourself in difficulties – but don't be afraid to claim the knowledge you do have and establish your credibility by the quality of your work and analysis.

TRUTH AND LIES

Generally it is best to avoid telling the court who or what to believe – that is the court's job and it needs no help on that score. Even if you are clear that someone has lied to you, generally it is best to state the facts and let the court draw its own conclusions as to who is telling the truth. However, if your belief that, for example, the parents lied to you affects your recommendations, it is important to explain this to the court as that belief forms part of your professional analysis. But take care not to jump to conclusions – lying does not necessarily imply guilt. Judges sometimes refer to a case[16] in which the then Lord Chief Justice discussed lies. The first question, then, is whether it really is a deliberate lie:

> If I am sure that a witness has lied then I must ask myself, why have they done so? A person may lie for many reasons and they may possibly be 'innocent' ones, for example, to bolster a true case; to protect somebody else, out of shame, panic, distress or confusion; or out of a wish to conceal disgraceful behaviour from their family. I remind myself that a lie told by a person can only strengthen or support evidence against that person if I am satisfied that (a) the lie was deliberate; (b) it relates to a material issue; and (c) there is no innocent explanation for it.

Occasionally the court may need expert assistance in understanding a child's testimony, such as explaining the nuances of a child's body language on video or interpreting his behaviour, and this may extend to advising the court on the child's credibility, but it must truly be expert evidence and not simply an account of who or what you believe.

---

16   *Lord Lane CJ in R v Lucas* [1981] 1 QB 720.

QUESTION FOR REFLECTION

- Are you an expert? If so, what are you an expert in? What are the limits of your expertise?

FOUNDATIONS OF EXPERT OPINIONS

Opinions and conclusions must always be based on the factual evidence to which the expert has applied his learning and experience. Facts and opinions should therefore be closely intertwined and it should be clear how one flows from the other.

As a professional working with the child and family, you have a dual role. You provide some of the core factual evidence on which the whole case is based, and you also offer opinions and recommendations which flow from your own observations. If you are the key worker, you also take into account the information you have received from others.

Your duty is to be balanced and objective, despite the fact that you are arguing for a particular outcome. You cannot pick only the facts which suit your conclusion and conveniently ignore the rest.

QUALITY OF ANALYSIS

At the same time as endorsing the role of social workers as experts, the courts have also been trenchant in their criticism of inadequate analysis and reasoning by some social workers. This has come to a head in cases where the care plan is adoption which, as the most drastic order available to the Family Court, brings the question into sharp relief. In one such case Munby P[17] expressed

> real concerns, shared by other judges, about the recurrent inadequacy of the analysis and reasoning put forward in support of the case for adoption, both in the materials put before the court by local authorities and guardians and also in too many judgments. This is nothing new. But it is time to call a halt.

When you are reaching your conclusions and recommendations for the child, McFarlane LJ[18] advised a 'global, holistic evaluation of each of the options for the child' instead of a linear analysis:

> what is required is a balancing exercise in which each option is evaluated to the degree of detail necessary to analyse and weigh

---

17   *Re B-S (Children)* [2013] EWCA 1146 (Court of Appeal).
18   *G (A Child)* [2013] EWCA Civ 965 paras 49–51.

its own internal positives and negatives and each option is then compared, side by side, against the competing option or options.[19]

This has led to references to a 'balance sheet' style analysis. If proper analysis is missing, the case is fundamentally flawed. In one case which went to the Court of Appeal, the local authority's statements were described as 'poor' and 'devoid of any welfare analysis' with insufficient justification for the plan for adoption outside the family. Ryder LJ explained:

> Where there is no welfare analysis of the realistic options before the court and/or no balance of the realistic options and no evaluation of the proportionality of the interference proposed, then...the decision making is flawed on the basis that the interference with article 8 of the Convention *[the right to family life]* has not been justified.

In that case, the court did not have enough information to carry out the welfare analysis and evaluation, so the care and placement orders were set aside and the case had to go back to court for re-hearing.

It is important to note that the 'balance sheet' style analysis requires just that – analysis – not simply running through a checklist of possible options and stating an opinion as to whether each is suitable or not. Careful reasoning is required.

Sir James Munby P said:[20]

> Most experienced family judges will unhappily have had too much exposure to material as anodyne and inadequate as that described... This sloppy practice must stop. It is simply unacceptable in a forensic context where the issues are so grave and the stakes, for both child and parent, so high.

We are at a critical moment for the social work profession. The courts are ready and willing to accept social workers as experts and to rely on their recommendations. The profession must now show that it is up to the job.

---

19   *Re G* at para. 54.
20   *Re B-S (Children)* [2013] EWCA 1146 (Court of Appeal).

Building a case

Together with your legal adviser, when you approach a case you should consider step by step how to construct your application and evidence. The following questions need to be considered.

Who has the burden of proof?

If these are care proceedings, the burden rests squarely on the local authority.

What is the standard of proof?

In care proceedings, this is the balance of probabilities.

What are the statutory grounds for your application?[21]

The key Children Act 1989 sections to remember for care proceedings are s38 (interim orders); s31 (threshold criteria for final orders); s1 (welfare principle, welfare checklist, no delay principle and the so-called 'no order principle'); not forgetting all relevant Articles under the Human Rights Act 1998 (especially Article 8, the right to respect for family life), as well as relevant provisions for any applications you are making under the Adoption and Children Act 2002 (such as a placement order application). Reminding yourself of the statutory grounds helps to focus your mind on what evidence you need to make out your case.

Exactly what is your case to the court in respect of each child individually? Is it a case of actual or likely harm? Precisely what type of harm do you allege? Remember that the grounds must be proven separately in respect of each child – children do not come as a 'job lot'.

What evidence do you have to establish your case?

This is the point at which you need to go from generalised allegations to very specific information illustrating each point. When preparing your case, it can help to create a chart or list setting out the allegation, information to support it and where the evidence comes from.

---

21 See Appendix 1 for a brief summary of the most important legal provisions in care proceedings.

Extract from chart – general neglect case		
Allegation	**Supporting information**	**Source**
Inadequate clothing	Child in T-shirt and nappy on snowy day	Keyworker
Inadequate nutrition	Observations of mealtimes	Social work assistant
Developmental delay	Developmental assessment	Community paediatrician

Who do you have to ask to give evidence, and what kind of evidence can they give?

Who do you need to provide pieces of the jigsaw? Consider everyone involved with the child and family. Agencies might include health (midwives, health visitors, GPs, hospital doctors), education (school teachers, school nurses, teaching assistants, playgroup or nursery staff), police, probation, youth offending teams (YOT), adult services (drug or alcohol services, mental health professionals). What factual and opinion evidence can they give? In most cases it should be clear from Case Conferences what information each agency has to contribute. Be sure to contact colleagues from other agencies as soon as possible – nobody appreciates being asked to prepare evidence at short notice except in a genuine emergency.

Do you need to gather any more evidence before the final hearing?

What else do you need to do? Are further assessments or other input needed? In spite of careful preparation before starting proceedings, some cases require further or ongoing work during the court process. Remember also to gather updated evidence demonstrating developments as the case progresses, and include evidence from people involved since the case started, such as foster carers and contact supervisors.

Is there a need for an expert to carry out a specific assessment for court?

Consider whether your authority needs to instruct someone, or how you would respond to another party seeking an expert opinion. (For further discussion of expert evidence *see* Chapter 8.)

QUESTIONS FOR REFLECTION

- How can you ensure that you present a rigorous analysis of the case to the court? Is it possible for your authority to devise any templates or checklists to help?

- How can you foster inter-agency co-operation to ensure that all relevant evidence is available?

Chapter 5

Written Evidence

The importance of written work

When we think about going to court, it is easy to focus on the drama of the day itself, but in fact court work starts long before anyone steps into the witness box. The application and evidence are submitted in writing in advance and are read by the court before anyone gives oral evidence. Presenting your written material well gives you the best chance of persuading the court of the merits of your case, so you owe this to your authority, to the child and to yourself. Of course, even immaculate presentation of a poor case cannot disguise its weakness – but bad presentation can undermine even a good case.

Cases which are soundly based and well presented often settle, ending by a negotiated agreement (which must of course be approved by the court). This saves everyone the stress, time and expense of a court contest. Even if the whole case is not resolved, some witnesses may be excused attendance because their evidence is sufficiently clear from their statements and cross-examination is not required, so by presenting your written work well you may even spare yourself the need to go into the witness box.

If you do have to be called, you give yourself the best start as a witness if you have produced a professional statement. Imagine for a moment a magistrate faced with lever arch files full of documents shortly before a fully contested hearing. It is a daunting task to absorb the information and, being human, he probably has other things he would rather be doing. He comes to the social worker's statement and finds a rambling, disorganised mess which is repetitive, badly presented, difficult to read, full of spelling mistakes and grammatical errors. He is quite likely to abandon it and turn straight to the Guardian's report.

When he does plough his way through it, imagine what impression he forms of the social worker and how he feels towards her when she steps into the witness box. In contrast, a statement which is clear, concise, well thought-out, logically organised and immaculately presented not only helps the magistrate understand the case but also means that he is well-disposed towards the social worker before she even comes to court. This can also go towards building a reputation from one case to another – just as you remember the magistrates, they may remember you.

Key considerations

Deadlines

Any document you produce for court must be on time. As soon as proceedings are underway, a timetable is fixed and deadlines are set for evidence to be filed (delivered to the court) and served (copied to the other parties). This timetable forms part of a court order and must be complied with, ever more so given the statutory time limit on care proceedings and the imperative to complete cases quickly for the sake of the children involved.

If for a good reason you really cannot keep to a deadline, tell your lawyer in advance so that he can seek an extension of time from the court. Too often, local authority evidence is filed late, and this has a knock-on effect as responses to your evidence are then delayed, and things end up being filed in a rush before the final hearing. It is not the correct way to do things and, unsurprisingly, courts take a dim view of local authorities which behave in this way and can make a costs order against the local authority. (See Chapter 8 for Munby P's emphatic comments on the need for court directions to be obeyed.)

Some people (including experts) have such a reputation for being late with their reports that solicitors have been known to give them the wrong date, 'accidentally' bringing the deadline forward by a couple of weeks in the hope of getting the report in on time. Avoid gaining such a reputation yourself.

Being late with evidence makes you and your authority look unprofessional and disorganised and is also disrespectful to the court. Remember that you are not the only person under pressure in the proceedings – other parties need as much time as possible to absorb your evidence – think, for example, of the illiterate parent for whom everything has to be read out, or a parent with mental health or emotional difficulties, who needs time to take in the information. If professionals cannot stick to a timetable, what chance do the parents have?

Remember too that other people, including your lawyer, need to check over your evidence before it can be filed and served, so aim to have your work finished at least a few days before it is due in. As soon as directions are given, diarise not just the date your work is due at court, but the date by which it needs to be finished. Put a note in your diary a week, a fortnight and a month before to remind you that the deadline is approaching. Make sure your managers give your court work the priority it deserves.

QUESTION FOR REFLECTION

- What habits can you adopt to ensure your work is always on time?

Accuracy

This may seem too obvious to mention, but it is too crucial to omit. Nothing should go into your statement unless you know it to be accurate and truthful. You have to swear to its truth in the witness box and anything untrue could lead to injustice and even to perjury proceedings and any number of disciplinary consequences. Don't guess; don't write what you think to be the case without bothering to check. Get it right. If your statement contains errors and inaccuracies, however minor, your credibility and reputation fly swiftly out of the window.

Audience

Consider who will read your work. Whether you are conscious of it or not, you already adjust your writing to its intended audience and purpose – a letter to your Mum is very different from a letter to your bank manager. The people who will read your evidence include:

- your own lawyer, who checks it and refines it to ensure that the case is made out and pitfalls avoided

- the other parties' lawyers, who go through it with a fine-tooth comb looking for gaps, weaknesses, inconsistencies, errors and anything which assists their case

- the other parties themselves, including the parents, who read in detail about their own family and failings

- the Children's Guardian, who analyses your work from a professional standpoint

- the child himself, immediately if he is old enough to take part in the proceedings, or perhaps later when he tries to understand his history

- the court – judge or magistrates – who look for clear evidence and cogent reasoning on which to base the decision.

Think about each of these people when you write and review your statements and reports. How will each of them read it? What will they see in it? Is that what you want them to see?

Presentation and style
This is discussed in Chapter 6.

Types of document
Before you draft anything, having a clear idea of its function helps you to produce an effective document. The details of the procedures and required documentation set out in the PLO are discussed in detail in Chapter 8, but in outline, they are as follows:

Application form
This sets out all the basic information for the case, including, crucially, a brief summary (no more than two pages long) setting out exactly why and how the local authority says that the grounds for care proceedings are met.

Social work chronology
This is filed at the outset of the proceedings, and is updated as the case goes along. It is a skeleton diary of events and should be succinct,

identifying key facts on which everyone can agree. It should not contain opinion or judgment; interpretation or analysis should be in a statement, not the chronology. It is effectively a schedule listing dates and events, and if possible should cross-reference to other statements or documents filed. The PLO defines[1] the chronology as a schedule containing:

***

Social Work Chronology

(a) A succinct summary of the length of involvement of the local authority with the family and in particular with the child.

(b) A succinct summary of the significant dates and events in the child's life in chronological order – i.e. a running record up to the issue of the proceedings; providing such information under the following headings:

(i) serial number

(ii) date

(iii) event-detail

(iv) witness or document reference (where applicable).

***

Assessments

These are documents which you produce anyway, independent of court proceedings, following a child protection referral and investigation, and the latest assessment must be filed at the commencement of proceedings. There is a danger of the same information being repeated *ad nauseam* between the various documents put before the court. Try to avoid this – repetition bores the reader and tempts him to skim-read, bringing the danger that he will skip over something original and important. Instead, cross-reference from one document to another; for example, if the core assessment contains a detailed family history, there is no need to repeat the whole thing in your statement. You could

---

1   *Family Procedure Rules* 2010 Practice Direction 12A para. 7.1 (Interpretation).

instead summarise the essentials and refer the reader to the relevant section of the assessment for fuller information.

Care plans

The initial care plan must be filed at the beginning of proceedings, with a final care plan to follow. Care plans are required by s31A Children Act 1989 and must follow regulations and statutory guidance.[2] When deciding whether to make a care order, the court must consider the permanence provisions,[3] that is, the plan for the child's long term placement, including timescales and a contingency plan if the first choice cannot be achieved.

The quality and robustness of the plan are crucial. In practice some care plans seem too formulaic, with identical plans for different children apparently cut and pasted from one to the other with little thought for the individual child. Each plan should be individual and specific, setting out your authority's realistic intentions for the particular child.

QUESTION FOR REFLECTION

- How can you use a standard format yet produce an individualised piece of work?

Statements of evidence

Parties and witnesses file statements of evidence, whereas experts and the Guardian file reports. You are likely to file at least two statements during the case. The initial social work statement has to be produced at the very outset of proceedings, and there may be further interim statements before the final statement. These contain the detailed evidence and analysis in support of your application and explain your recommendation to the court.

---

2   *Care Planning, Placement and Case Review (England) Regulations 2010* and *The Children Act 1989 Guidance and Regulations Volume 2: Care Planning, Placement and Case Review*, HM Gov 2010, available at www.gov.uk/government/publications/children-act-1989-care-planning-placement-and-case-review, accessed on 25 August 2014.

3   s15 Children and Families Act 2014.

Social work statements

Obviously the precise content depends on the detail of your particular case and you need to work closely with your lawyer to get this right. You also need to be clear about your role in the case – are you a witness of fact or are you also qualified to give opinions? Are you giving evidence about a discrete piece of work, such as contact observation, or are you the key worker putting forward the case as a whole? If your evidence just relates to one piece of work, stick to that and do not stray beyond your boundaries. The rest of this section applies primarily to the key worker.

PLO requirements

The PLO specifies the requirements for a social work statement.[4] This should be closely followed in each case.

Social Work Statement

'Social Work Statement' means a statement prepared by the Local Authority limited to the following evidence:

Summary

(a) the order sought

(b) succinct summary of reasons with reference as appropriate to the Welfare Checklist

Family

(c) family members and relationships especially the primary carers and significant adults/other children

(d) genogram

---

4   *Family Procedure Rules 2010* Practice Direction 12A para. 7.1 (Interpretation).

Threshold

   (e) precipitating events

      (i) background circumstances: summary of children's services involvement cross-referenced to the chronology

      (ii) previous court orders and emergency steps

   (f) previous assessments summary of significant harm and or likelihood of significant harm which the LA will seek to establish by evidence or concession

Parenting capability

   (g) assessment of child's needs

   (h) assessment of parental capability to meet needs

   (i) analysis of why there is a gap between parental capability and the child's needs

   (j) assessment of other significant adults who may be carers

Child impact

   (k) wishes and feelings of the child(ren)

   (l) timetable for the child

   (m) delay and timetable for the proceedings

Permanence and contact

   (n) parallel planning

   (o) realistic placement options by reference to a welfare and proportionality analysis

   (p) contact framework

Case management

   (q) evidence and assessments necessary and outstanding

(r) any information about any person's litigation capacity, mental health issues, disabilities or vulnerabilities that is relevant to their capability to participate in the proceedings, and

(s) case management proposals.

In some cases, proceedings start after long, exhaustive work with the family; assessments are complete and the court can be given a full picture from the outset. Other cases begin with an emergency where you have little or no previous knowledge of the family. Then your initial statement is necessarily sparse and can only give the information available to date, including as much detail as possible on the incident which propelled you to court, any emergency action taken, other known court cases or orders relating to the child, and such background as you have on the family, including your initial assessment.

If your plan involves removing the child from home, an initial care plan is also needed, with as much detail as possible as to placement and contact. You may be facing a contested interim care hearing, so you need to be very clear about your reasoning justifying the need for an interim order and removal from home.

At all times, think about what the court needs to know. If you were the judge, what would you want to see in the statement?

Be clear at the outset what your application is and what order(s) (interim or final) you seek. This is not a thriller where you build up the suspense to the end before revealing your application. Your reasoning and analysis come later, but stating early on exactly what you seek allows the court and other parties to read your statement in context. This will also remind you to refer to the relevant legal provisions and criteria throughout to make sure that your evidence is properly focused.

Qualifications and experience

Start your first statement with your full name and professional address (of course you should never reveal your personal contact details), and job title (including a very brief explanation if necessary). Give your qualifications and experience to establish your entitlement to give opinion evidence. Some pre-qualification experience and other activities can be included if relevant. Some witnesses overdo it, including membership of organisations for which only a subscription is required – no one is fooled by this and it tends to undermine the value of the other entries in the list. A long list of letters after your name does not assist the court either – be prepared to explain those which are not obvious.

Do not trawl through your full details in every statement you write for the same case – this wastes time and energy and no one will read it a second time. After the first statement just give your name and address and refer to the details of your qualifications and experience in your first statement, giving its date. Do, however, add details if you have subsequently been promoted or obtained a further qualification.

Details of your role

State your role with the family and consider including a brief explanation of what this actually entails, how often you visit and how you work. Social workers sometimes complain that they are given less credence than the Guardian even though they know the child and family better. This may be because they are not giving the court enough information. In their reports, Guardians detail every interview undertaken and are precise about who they have seen and when, but social workers rarely do so and are not always able to answer if asked for the same details. Can you say how often you have visited a family you are working with or how long you have spent with the child? If not, why not? Support your claim to know the family well by including details in your statement. This was important in one interim hearing where the Guardian disagreed with the local authority's application. The social worker believed that the Guardian did not have a true picture of the family, who had put on a show for her, and that the child had not told her his real feelings. The social worker was able to tell the court that she had worked with the family intensively over three months, clocking up 24 hours with the parents and a further 18 hours with the child individually. In contrast, the Guardian had spent a total of 1½ hours with the family and had seen the child once. The court preferred the social worker's evidence.

Information about the child

Make sure that you include all relevant details about the child's background and characteristics. Once, a judge who had read all of the papers before a first hearing was surprised to see a black mother and white father in court – the child's mixed racial heritage appeared nowhere in the papers. When you work closely on a case, it is sometimes easy to overlook what seems obvious to you – don't forget the court does not know unless you tell it.

Try to convey a picture of each child as an individual person. It is too easy for paper-based professionals (such as lawyers and judges) to regard the child as simply the subject of the proceedings, an object of concern or a collection of evidence, not an individual. We focus on what has happened to the child and his problems, and rarely get a glimpse of personality, let alone talents or interests. It is also too easy to consider all of the children of the family together, without making key distinctions between the separate individual children in the case.

Remember also always to bring the evidence back to the child – too often cases focus on adults, the local authority concentrating on the parents' inadequacies and the parents complaining about the local authority. The only reason why any of the information about the parents' background, lifestyle or behaviour is relevant is because of its impact on the child, whose welfare is paramount. Sometimes it is useful to remind yourself why you are putting information in. The mother's heroin addiction is there not because society disapproves of drug use, or even because it is harming her health – the only reason it matters to you or the court is because it harms her child.

Paternity

Identify at an early stage who is who in the child's life. Make it clear who the parents are and who has PR, remembering that these are not necessarily the same (it is possible to be a parent without PR and to have PR without being a parent). Never overlook the child's father even if he does not live with the family. If he has PR, he is automatically a party to the proceedings and must be served with all the papers. Even if he does not have PR, he cannot be ignored – some cases have gone right through to adoption proceedings before the putative father has been contacted, only to find he or his family want to care for the child, causing delay and trauma to all concerned. Tell the court what you know about the child's paternity and what efforts you have made or will make to track the father down. If there is any doubt, DNA testing is now cheap, simple and effective. Remember also that if there are several children, there may also be several different fathers to consider.

Siblings

Siblings and half-siblings must not be overlooked. Care planning can become complex particularly where large age gaps, different parentage or other considerations lead to different plans for siblings, and these issues should be identified early on.

Supporting evidence

As explained in Chapter 4, the authority must provide evidence for each of its allegations to illustrate and justify its case. Make sure your case stands up to robust scrutiny. Use direct evidence, not hearsay, whenever possible. As key worker, you can pull together evidence from statements from other witnesses (without repeating all the detail) to show how the case fits together as a whole.

Make sure you convey your key points clearly and that the balance is right. Important issues must be given appropriate detail and emphasis; trivial points might be left out altogether. Sometimes the balance is wrong – one statement mentioned a child's worryingly sexualised behaviour in one sentence, but spent a page and a half on the dangers of passive smoking. In another case of gross neglect the social worker complained in her statement that the mother had not washed her curtains. This had no relevance to the threshold criteria and, frankly, dirty curtains were the least of the child's worries. It does not help to throw in every single criticism of the parent or family – in fact it gives the impression either of muddled thinking ('this worker doesn't know what's important') or judgmental hyper-criticism ('this poor mother can't do anything right'). Does it really matter? Can the child stay at home even if her parents continue to smoke, or if the curtains are chronically unclean? Focus on what really needs to change.

Give specific examples and illustrations, avoiding generalised comments and subjective judgments (words like 'unacceptable' or 'inappropriate') or vague words like 'issues' or 'concerns'. Once a social worker discussing potential proceedings explained to her lawyer that there were concerns about the home conditions. The lawyer asked for clarification. The worker explained that the hygiene standards were unacceptable. The lawyer asked for facts not an opinion. The discussion continued in the same vein until the worker, exasperated, said, 'Look, the other day I went in and the sink was full of washing-up with a dishcloth on top. Mother took the dishcloth, wiped the baby's bottom then put the cloth back in the sink.' At last the lawyer was happy – with factual evidence like that, the magistrates could work out for themselves that this was poor hygiene practice without the help of expert social work opinion. Paint the picture for the court – don't forget the magistrates will never visit the home, meet the child or see the family in action.

Give detailed observations of family interactions, rather than simply expressing a view of the strength of attachments – show the court where you get your opinions from. Remember that opinions are only valid if they relate to facts.

Consider whether to attach anything to your statement; this is known as an 'exhibit'. If you have referred to a written agreement, attach a copy. If you have gone through a workbook or have produced charts, daily programmes, lists of targets or any other tool in your work with the family, consider whether a copy would help the court. Don't forget photographs or evidence other than the written word.

Balance

You swear to tell the court the whole truth – not just the bits of the truth which suit your case. The local authority must give the court the full picture, and not drive forward towards its desired conclusion, presenting information selectively.

Judges have often stressed the importance of balance. For example Wall J (who later became President of the Family Division of the High Court) said:[5]

> All parties have a duty in family proceedings not to be tendentious in the presentation of their evidence. That duty is, however, particularly acute in relation to local authority evidence, and never more so than when the local authority is advising the court of its view of the outcome of an assessment of parental capacity or otherwise setting out its recommendations and plans. The duty of local authorities to be objective, fair and balanced cannot be overemphasised.

If you fail to heed this advice, the parents' advocates will inevitably cross-examine you to elicit all of their clients' positive qualities. The next question is why none of these were in your statement. If you have left out these important matters, what else have you also conveniently

---

5   In *Re J C* [1995] 2 FLR 77 High Court at p80D.

omitted to mention? You are made to look biased, judgmental and selective – not a witness the court would choose to trust. Far better, therefore, to be fair and balanced throughout.

Although we can all think of a few clients about whom it is a struggle to find positive comments, most families have strengths as well as weaknesses and although the negatives may outweigh the positives, both need to be stated.

QUESTION FOR REFLECTION

- How can you be sure always to achieve the right balance while addressing positives as well as negatives in your statements?

Local authority involvement

The court needs to know what your department and other agencies have done to try to improve things. This goes towards explaining why an order is necessary. Just as the parents are not without redeeming features, it is unlikely that the agencies are beyond reproach. Imagine a hypothetical case where timely action has not been taken, the case has languished unallocated, a service was unavailable due to lack of resources or in some other way your department has failed to cover itself with glory. How do you handle it? Essentially you have two options: say nothing and hope that no one notices, or tackle it head on.

If you say nothing, how likely is it that the lawyers and the court will all miss the point? If one of them does take the matter up, you will immediately be on the defensive, looking as if you had tried to hide something, and again the implication arises that there might be other things you have conveniently omitted. It looks as though the barrister has winkled information out of you, and has scored a point. He will make a meal of it. Your confidence will be undermined and your department's credibility damaged.

In contrast, if you tackle the issue yourself, acknowledging the failings in your statement (without blowing them out of proportion), apologising if necessary, then moving on, you are demonstrably being frank with the court and fair to all parties.

There is nothing wrong with acknowledging, for example, that, with hindsight, there might have been grounds for proceedings long ago but they were not taken through a desire, perhaps misplaced, to keep the child at home if at all possible. The fact that it could be argued that action should have been taken earlier is not a reason to compound the error by continuing to fail to act. What can the other parties do with their criticism now? They can still make the same points, but much of the sting has been drawn. Their criticisms are not original, and the social worker can refer to the acknowledgment already in her statement. By so doing, she clearly shows her honesty and fairness, and is likely to win the court's respect.

Analysis and opinion

As explained in Chapter 4, the court needs expert analysis of the facts and a fully worked and reasoned opinion. Just stating a conclusion or a recommendation is not enough – you must be able to explain and justify your opinion and your authority's application.

Research

Social workers often ask whether they should refer in evidence to research or the theoretical basis for their opinions. Practice is increasingly research-and evidence-based, and is part of the drive to increase the professionalism of social work.

Nonetheless, take care before you cite research or theory. Ask yourself whether it is necessary at all – most care cases proceed without it. Is the point so unusual and technical that it needs to be justified? Have you actually used the research or theory in your work with the child? If not, it is no good producing it just for court to look more professional – you will regret it when it comes to cross-examination. Always consider how the research or theory relates to this child and this family; generalisations do not assist the court.

If you do consider it essential, be very careful. Make sure it is authoritative, generally accepted and up-to-date. One problem is that whatever research you cite, someone else will find a study supporting the opposite proposition, and that 'someone else' is quite likely to be the parents' barrister. You therefore need to know if there are any contradictory opinions and to be able to explain why you discount them.

Make sure any theoretical work you rely on is sound and respectable – just as with any other expert, if you take a view which is not generally accepted within your profession, you must acknowledge that upfront;

court is not a place to crusade for unorthodox or innovative beliefs. Work-funded research or that published by government departments or well-known institutions is likely to be safe – your friend's doctoral thesis is not.

Beware of the internet. In one case, a research paper was produced, obtained from the internet, propounding an original theory that would explain a child's medical symptoms. When the source was investigated, it transpired that the writer did indeed have a doctorate – but in geography – and other papers on the same site included accounts of alien abductions. If you do find information to support your case, follow it up, authenticate it and analyse it – imagine the questions a sharp, well-informed lawyer will ask and make sure you have the answers. Other parties can ask for a copy of anything you rely on, so make sure you can provide it at short notice or, better still, supply it in advance. If (and only if) research really is necessary, and you present it properly, it could add to your credibility as a witness – but do it carelessly and you will undermine your own professionalism. Avoid at all costs generalised statements such as, 'We know from research…' – that is simply asking for trouble.

Conclusion

Written work is the foundation of evidence in the Family Court. It is important to get it right. You may find it helpful to use the statement checklist in Appendix 2 to review your own statements, as well as those of other witnesses.

Chapter 6

Statement Presentation

Presentation matters

Deciding on the content of your statement is half the battle; you then need to get the information across effectively. This includes using the right format, organising the material and expressing yourself clearly and appropriately.

Format

There are formal requirements for court documents and complying with these is essential for professional presentation.

All statements for the court must contain a statement of truth,[1] saying quite simply, 'I believe that the facts stated in this witness statement are true'. This declaration must be signed by the person making the statement. If this is not done, the court could rule the evidence in the statement inadmissible. The witness must sign in her own name, not that of her employing agency or authority. Of course it is a serious matter if a witness signs a statement containing a false statement without honestly believing it to be true. This could lead to proceedings for perjury, which in turn could lead to imprisonment.

Practice Direction 22A provides that the statement must be headed with the title of the proceedings. It then goes on to list detailed requirements for a statement before the Family Court.

---

1   Part 17 *Family Procedure Rules 2010.*

Practice Direction 22A

3.2

...at the top right-hand corner of the first page (and on the backsheet) there should be clearly written:

(a) the party on whose behalf it is made

(b) the initials and surname of the maker

(c) the number of the affidavit/statement in relation to its maker

(d) the identifying initials and number of each exhibit referred to, and

(e) the date made.

3.3

The affidavit/statement should:

(a) be produced on durable quality A4 paper with a 3.5 cm margin

(b) be fully legible and should normally be typed on one side of the paper only

(c) where possible, should be bound securely in a manner which would not hamper filing...

(d) have the pages numbered consecutively as a separate document (or as one of several documents contained in a file)

(e) be divided into numbered paragraphs

(f) have all numbers, including dates, expressed in figures, and

(g) give the reference to any document or documents mentioned either in the margin or in bold text in the body of the affidavit/statement.

Never forget the case number. Children's cases are always classified by their numbers and names are not read out in order to preserve confidentiality. Get the number wrong and the document may never reach the correct file.

The rules prescribe the use of A4 paper with single-sided text. The requirement for margins is a practical one – you need to allow space so that the statement can be photocopied and hole-punched without chopping off part of the text. Participants in the case may also want to write notes on their copy of the statement.

Use at least one and a half line spacing. Number all paragraphs and keep the paragraphs a manageable length – you will be grateful for this when you are referred to the text in the witness box – it is much easier to find 'paragraph 5' than 'the 23rd line, about three-quarters of the way down the page', especially when you are nervous! Keep the numbering style consistent throughout. If you start with 1(a) and (b), don't suddenly change to 2.1 part-way through.

Formal requirements

Practice Direction 22A provides that a statement should start with the maker's full name and (in the case of evidence given in a professional capacity) professional address, position held, occupation, employer's name and employer's status as a party to the proceedings (in care proceedings the local authority is the applicant).

The statement must make clear which information is from the witness's own knowledge and which are matters of information and belief, in which case the source of the information must be identified.

The prescribed contents for social work chronologies and statements have been outlined in Chapter 5.

Organisation

You have a lot of important information to convey in a limited space. It can only be accessible if it is well organised. Consider the judge and the other parties. They need to be able to read the statement through from beginning to end and make sense of it, but also to find their way to relevant information when they need it. Imagine that, in the heat of the hearing, a witness says something untrue (for example, the mother says she attended a particular meeting whereas your statement says she did not). It is no good having your advocate fumbling around thinking 'I know I read that somewhere'; he needs to be able to turn straight to the details in your statement to challenge her evidence, so a clear structure is crucial.

Making information accessible

Give yourself 15 seconds each to read A and B. Which do you prefer?

A. It might be possible to argue that the layout and appearance of a statement should not be considered as particularly important; rather that the content of the statement is the only significant matter. Arguably, however, the problem is that the content of the statement can only be appreciated if the reader can actually read and absorb it. If the page is too tightly packed with small, closely spaced verbiage lacking any divisions which might assist the reader by separating the text into manageable sections and failing to provide headings which might help in anticipating and understanding the main topics and structure of the statement, and if the text consists of very long sentences, repetitions and unnecessary verbiage, as well as multiple sub-clauses which are simply too complex and serve only to obscure the content of the sentence, set within extremely long paragraphs, then ultimately the sense of the text becomes lost and the effort put into writing the statement becomes wasted as the meaning is obscured. It can actually be physically difficult and tiring to read if the writing is too small and too closely packed together, especially when this continues for page after page. It can even be difficult to follow the sense of the writing, and sometimes one can get the feeling that the writer him or herself has actually got lost, followed inevitably by the reader! If the reader has to read a sentence or a paragraph more than once to try to find the sense of it, then the writer has wasted his or her time. The chances are that the reader will not make the effort to keep on trying and will move on. If the sentence or paragraph had obscured within it important information, then that information itself is passed over Further, it is simply unappealing and does not entice the reader, who may already be reluctant, tired or bored, to want to read the text and he or she will be encouraged to skim over all or part of the text or alternatively to find another statement (or perhaps the Guardian's report) to read instead. Surprising as it may seem to many, judges and magistrates are in fact human, and do not differ greatly from other readers. It is difficult to justify writing a statement in a way which makes life more difficult for the reader or in a way which the writer him or herself would in fact be reluctant to read were the positions reversed.

B. The layout of a statement is important because its content will only be noticed if it is accessible. Possible problems with statements include:

- font inappropriate and/or too small

- line spacing too close

- lack of sub-divisions and headings

- unnecessarily complex sentences

- excessively long paragraphs.

Small writing is difficult and tiring to read. Complex sentences can obscure the meaning and bore the reader. Large blocks of dense text are unattractive and discourage the reader. Why write a statement you would not want to read yourself?

Social work statements can sometimes read like amplified chronologies and simply trawl through every single contact with the family and every step taken, in great detail. This makes turgid reading and leaves the reader to do the work in figuring out the significance of each event. Although Practice Direction 22A paragraph 4.4 says that 'it is usually convenient to follow the chronological sequence of events or matters dealt with', this is advisory rather than compulsory. Given that, as the key social worker, you will already have filed a social work chronology, it may sometimes be better to organise the information by topics rather than dates. Lists or bullet points can make points more clearly than long screeds of text.

Headings and sub-headings give structure to your statement, breaking up the text into manageable chunks and providing helpful signposting for the reader. Put all your points about the same topic in the same section.

Use different typefaces for clarification, such as bold for headings or italics for quotations. Sentences should be of a manageable length, without too many sub-clauses. This is in your own interests, as well as those of your readers, because if you are referred to your statement in the witness box, you will live to regret long and complex sentences. Experts in plain English recommend that sentences should generally contain one main point and should not be too long – aim for 40 words as a maximum and 15–20 words as an average. This makes the content more easily accessible. However, you do need to vary sentence length a little, or the statement will seem too staccato and will not flow. Collect sentences on the same topic into paragraphs, which also need to be of a sensible length.

Length

Social workers sometimes ask how long a statement should be. There is no easy answer; much, of course, depends on the characteristics of the particular case. There is also a question of personal style – some people are more concise than others and, even given the same facts and the same conclusion, no two people would write the same statement. You know whether you are naturally verbose or concise. If you tend to write too much, write a first draft then edit it. Always ask yourself why each piece of information you are giving is relevant – what does it add? Remove sentences which add nothing significant. The key is quality, not quantity.

Imagine you are packing for a plane journey with a strict baggage weight allowance: you probably over-pack to start with, then you prune, leaving behind the unnecessary items, reducing the number of similar things, or replacing several items altogether with a single more useful one. You can apply the same ideas to your writing.

If you need to become more concise, try practising a précis exercise. Take a passage of, say, 150 words from a book or journal and try to rewrite it in 100 words, or 50 words (the word count facility in word processing packages is a godsend). This sharpens the discipline of analysing the key points in the text, then expressing those ideas more economically, discarding the excess baggage along the way. You can then use these skills in your statement writing.

It is equally possible to be too brief and too sparse. Too little information can even be worse than being too long-winded. The waffler risks boring the reader and losing important points in a welter of unnecessary detail, but the taciturn writer could fail even to make the case or, if she adds further information in the witness box which was not in the statement, could be criticised for apparently trying to surprise the opposition with new information.

Sometimes a case which is long and complex requires a long and complex statement – as Einstein put it, '[m]ake it as simple as possible, but no simpler'.

Language

Language should be formal but plain and clear – use ordinary English words without patronising your audience. Avoid jargon and be prepared to explain any specialist terms you do use. However, don't lose sight of common sense – the health visitor service which appended a 'glossary of specialist terms' to statements really did not need to explain that 'pregnancy' was a term meaning 'the period of gestation of the foetus prior to birth'.

Use language which is natural to you, albeit the formal version of you – do not try to impress with your learning, and never use a word unless you are completely sure of its meaning. You could end up being cross-examined about why you have chosen a particular word or expressed yourself in a particular way and it is difficult to answer if you have written in a way which is unnatural to you or, even more so if you have not written the statement yourself. In one case where the social worker's evidence had been drafted for her by a lawyer, the worker found herself in the witness box being asked repeatedly about why she had used a particular term. She struggled gamely to answer the question several times but when it was posed yet again she gave up in exasperation, saying, 'I don't know, I didn't write it – she did!' and pointed to the lawyer at the back of the court.

Parents' solicitors have a difficult task preparing their clients' evidence. Most parents are not equipped to draft their own statements, so solicitors have do it for them, trying to get the parents' point across in language they might use, although sometimes with necessary editing! Occasionally parents' statements contain patent lawyer-speak, such as 'I have been informed and verily believe' or 'I deny each and every allegation made by the local authority and I put them to strict proof thereof.' Most advocates resist the temptation to cross-examine the parents on what they meant by those words.

Although your lawyer (or your supervisor) is unlikely to make such clumsy changes to your statement, words or sentences inserted by someone else might stand out because of a difference in style – for the reader, it can be almost as though another voice suddenly starts speaking. It is better for others to suggest the sense of the alteration and let you write it in your own words; indeed Practice Direction 22A paragraph 4.1[2] says that a statement 'must, if practicable be in the maker's own words'.

Guides to plain English generally advise writers to use the active ('the fostering officer will support the placement') rather than the passive voice ('the placement will be supported by the fostering officer'). Occasionally, social workers write in the third person, referring to themselves as 'the social worker' rather in the style of a doctoral thesis ('the writer will demonstrate…'). This can be unclear – for example, 'The social worker went to the house' raises the question of 'which

---

2   Available at www.justice.gov.uk/courts/procedurerules/family/practice_directions/ pd_part_22a, accessed on 25 August 2014.

social worker?' If it was in fact the statement writer who went, it sounds strange, perhaps pretentious or even giving the impression that the writer is trying to disown the action. One of the give-away signs that a worker does not agree with actions taken or decisions made is when she writes, for example, 'The Department decided', thereby distancing herself from the decision. It is far better and clearer to write about your own actions in the first person ('I went to the house'); indeed Practice Direction 22A paragraph 4.1 makes it clear that this is normal best practice.

Grammar and spelling

Our education system has not always laid great store on grammar or spelling, on occasions preferring to encourage self-expression. As a result, even some highly educated people make basic errors. Court proceedings are not English language exams, but spelling and grammar still matter. Mistakes can change the sense of a sentence. Look at the following two sentences – only the punctuation changes, but the sense is completely different:

The client said the social worker was a bitch.

'The client,' said the social worker, 'was a bitch.'

A statement which contains errors of whatever nature looks unprofessional. Remember your audience and bear in mind that judges in particular tend to come from a narrow social group often educated in a traditional manner, and, being lawyers, also tend to be pedantic.

Some people are driven to distraction by common grammatical errors such as the split infinitive ('to boldly go') or the greengrocers' (or is it greengrocer's?) apostrophe (pear's 30p). However irrational it may seem to those more relaxed about such things, some people presented with a statement full of such errors can barely see past them to the content.

If you are not confident about the difference between 'it's' and 'its', 'parents', 'parent's' and 'parents'' or 'there', 'their' and 'they're', the office assistant on your computer may help, but remember that the computer is no substitute for a thinking human being – ask a colleague well-versed in grammar to check your work for you, and consider brushing up your skills.

Names

When you write about adults, as a general rule you should use their title and surname, at least on the first occasion. This shows an appropriate level of formality and respect for the individual concerned. If you find this artificial, you could, for example, write: 'The child's mother is Mrs Jane Smith, whom I will refer to in this statement as "Jane" as we work together on first name terms.' This explains to the court that you are not using her first name because you regard yourself as superior to her, and that she uses your first name as well.

Be aware that different cultures have different naming systems and do not always have a first name followed by a surname. Be particularly careful to get it right, and if in doubt, ask the people themselves for the correct form of address.

Be careful to differentiate if there is more than one family member with the same name.

Always take care to spell names correctly, particularly if the spellings are idiosyncratic. Many people are justifiably highly offended by mistakes in their name, and it does imply a lack of care and respect. Surnames can be a major bone of contention – many private law disputes centre on a child's surname, and courts take the issue of children's names very seriously – so make sure you get it right. Dates of birth also matter. Parents can become very upset about mistakes of this kind, even when they accept damning criticism of their behaviour without apparent demur. It can also put you on the back foot in the witness box, apologising for an error before you have even started, and what may seem a relatively minor matter can be blown out of all proportion, denting your confidence.

Avoid referring to parties as 'the mother/father' (unless you genuinely do not know their names). It comes across as dismissive, not to say plain rude.

Sensitivity

Remember that the people you are writing about (parents and children) are likely to read your work and, unlike others in the case, you will carry on working with them after the court proceedings are over. It is essential to be frank about events in the family and this necessarily involves raising sensitive issues, detailing very personal matters and analysing people's failings. These matters must be tackled head-on without pussy-footing around or you will not convey your concerns to the court. However, there is no need to be gratuitous or insensitive. For example, one report included the fact that the mother's false teeth fell out during an interview, an event which had no bearing on the case. Another report described a father as a 'psychosexual deviant' because he was gay. Expressing things in this way hardly assisted the court in its task and was unnecessarily hurtful to the individuals involved. Imagine also the impression of the writer this conveys to the court – is someone who writes like this a fair-minded, sensitive professional? How, then, has he worked with this family and what attitude has he taken towards them? How reliable are his recommendations to the court?

There is nothing at all wrong with expressing regret, sympathy or sadness in a statement, where appropriate. A case where the parents' inadequate care for the child is due to their learning disabilities is very different from a case of sadistic cruelty and it is perfectly proper for the statements to reflect this. In the first case, it is quite appropriate to comment, for example, that despite the parents' evident love for the child and the authority's efforts to support them, sadly they have proved unable to provide good enough care. The parents' pain and sadness at being separated from their child should be acknowledged. A statement does not have to be cold and impersonal to be professional.

Emotive language

A judge hearing a Guardian describe a case as the worst she had ever seen commented, 'Yes, it always is, isn't it?' The Guardian had said the same thing so many times that it was simply devalued, like the boy who cried 'wolf'. On the day when she was confronted with a truly awful situation, she had no words left to convey it.

Avoid overstatement and absolutes – be careful about 'always', 'never' or any sense of 100 per cent certainty. Words like 'appalling', 'disgusting', 'shocking' are emotional, emotive and subjective. They may tell the court more about the writer than about the situation described. You are not writing a novel; your aim is not to provoke an emotional response from the reader. If such words are to be used at all, they should be saved for truly exceptional situations which really merit them. Even then, sometimes cool understatement is more effective than emotive language. Read the Climbié report[3] and the descriptions of events. You will not find adjectives; they are not necessary. The bare facts say it all.

Tone

The same information can be expressed in countless ways, each with a different nuance; it is not just what you say, but how you say it that matters. The English language is particularly rich, having numerous synonyms and words with only subtly different meanings. A thesaurus can be very useful to help you find just the right word.

Always remember that the way you write not only conveys information about your subject matter, but also about you. Your readers form impressions of you and your practice, which they will take with them into court before you even set foot in the witness box.

---

3   Laming (2003) *The Victoria Climbié Inquiry: Report of an Inquiry by Lord Laming.* London: Stationery Office. Available at www.publications.parliament.uk/pa/cm200203/cmselect/cmhealth/570/570.pdf, accessed on 25 August 2014.

Choosing the right word

The following words could all be used to describe a 13-year-old. What different impressions do they convey? Which might you choose to use and why?

- child

- youth

- juvenile

- young person

- teenager

- adolescent

- schoolboy/girl

- youngster

- kid.

Reactions to the list vary, but some comments follow:

Child: This is legally correct as childhood lasts until 18. Most people, however, instinctively feel that 'child' refers to someone younger than 13. A worker might choose this word deliberately, for example, for a 13-year-old who appears streetwise and acts like an older teenager to remind everyone he is in fact a child. The same point might be made for a 13-year-old who has an inappropriate level of responsibility, caring for siblings or incapacitated parents.

Youth: If used as a noun ('a youth') people generally think male not female, and the tone is critical not positive – it implies trouble, as in 'a group of youths', conjuring up an image of a gang hanging around menacingly on a street corner. As an adjective, it might summon up 'youth court', but can also be positive, as in 'youth orchestra' or 'youth group'.

Juvenile: The universal reaction to this word is that it is negative in tone and masculine in gender.

Young person: Professionals like this term. It seems respectful of the individual, acknowledging his status as a person, just a youthful one. Some young people themselves, however, find it patronising (or, in the words of one teenage client, 'poncey'). It is an artificial term, not one the average person would use, and borders on jargon. Young woman/man or girl/boy might be more natural.

Teenager: Reactions to this are mixed. For a 13-year-old, becoming a teenager is an important milestone. Some, however, think of 'Kevin' (Harry Enfield's awkward teenage comic creation).

Adolescent: This often suggests a medical context (particularly child and adolescent mental health services) and does accurately label the phase between childhood and adulthood, but it also raises the spectre of hormones, mood swings and acne. It rarely conjures up a positive image.

Schoolboy/girl: Generally this creates an image of a younger child, and a picture of innocence. It is notable that often the media refer to child victims of crime as, for example, 'the murdered schoolgirl' even where there is no connection between the crime and school. It seems that this is precisely to convey the impression of innocence betrayed.

Youngster: Often this is thought to give the impression of an older speaker, although there are regional variations. Some people find it patronising, others consider it affectionate.

Kid: A word you might use informally but not in a report. For some this raises hackles, but this is how some young clients describe themselves.

So we can see that the choice of noun can convey a different picture of the same person.

Choosing the right tone

Here are three descriptions of the same person. What do they suggest to you?

1. John is a young person with a problem of drug use, leading to repeated involvement in criminal activity. He needs help with anger management.

2. John is a repeat offender and drug abuser with low impulse control.

3. John is a drug-addicted thug.

The three descriptions give similar information, but in very different ways. Example 1 takes care first to describe John as a young person before detailing his problems. The other two examples both label him by his behaviour. Example 1 identifies the underlying problem, then the consequence, then suggests assistance. Neither of the others suggests any constructive response to the situation.

Then there is the difference in language, example 1 being moderate and mild, example 2 using labels and straying into jargon (especially 'low impulse control'), whereas example 3 is colloquial.

It has been suggested that example 1 is what the social worker writes for care proceedings, 2 is for the Youth Court and 3 is what she says in the office; or that 1 is what you read in a social work journal, 2 in a broadsheet newspaper and 3 in a tabloid.

Perhaps the most notable difference, however, is the difference in tone between the three examples. As well as gaining some information about John, you have probably formed an impression of the author of each statement, her attitudes and approach.

So we can see that the way you express yourself in a statement can say as much about you as the situation you are describing.

Critical reading

Try reviewing statements you have written in the past, and consider statements produced by others. Read them critically – look at content, presentation, organisation, expression and tone – and think how they could be improved. The checklist in Appendix 2 might help.

Top ten writing tips

1. Make time to write

It is simply impossible to write a good statement in ten minutes snatched here and there between other appointments. You need to allow a good stretch of uninterrupted time to do justice to the task and to the child. Effectively, writing time has to be treated as any other professional commitment, such as a meeting or appointment. Strike the time out in your diary and ensure that both you and your colleagues treat this as sacrosanct, not a luxury.

2. Find space to write

You need a quiet space to work where you can concentrate uninterrupted. Some people work well at home, while others suddenly feel an overwhelming need to clean the oven – you know what works for you. Take care also to preserve confidentiality if you work at home, including computer security. If you have to work at the office find a quiet room. Some teams who have no option but to work in an open plan office use a 'traffic light' system, with red, amber and green symbols on their desks, indicating to colleagues what level of emergency justifies an interruption – writing a statement is definitely 'code red' (do not disturb except in case of fire).

3. Re-read your file

Before you start to write, refresh your memory of the file, including related files. This may be a lot of reading, but over time details fade from memory. Sometimes you will see a pattern when you look back over the whole story which was not apparent at the time, or you may gain a new perspective on a case you thought you already knew. Take the opportunity to ensure that your file is in good order and to flag up important pages ready for the court day.

4. Think

It sounds too obvious to mention but you need to be very clear in your own mind exactly what you want to say before you commit it to paper. Often we are so pressed, rushing from one appointment to the next, that we have little time for reflection. You cannot write coherently without first formulating your thoughts. Simple steps like sorting out in your own mind the three most important things that need to change to allow the child to stay at home can help.

5. Plan

Once you know what you want to say, the next stage is to plan how to say it. Time spent planning saves time writing, and if you try to write without planning, you are likely to produce an unstructured stream of consciousness. Refine your thinking – plan your structure and be clear of the major points you want to get across. Many people find it useful to write down their headings before they start on the content.

6. Get started

Procrastination is a common problem. Sometimes we say we haven't got time to do one thing yet manage to find time to do something else, so it can really come down to a question of priorities. Everyone appreciates that social workers have heavy workloads, but it is difficult to think of anything more important than proceedings which could determine a child's future. If you genuinely cannot find time for this important task, you have a more profound problem – either your workload is too heavy, or you are not coping effectively with it and need some support or training such as a time management course. Either way, you owe it to yourself and your clients to tackle this with your seniors.

Why do you procrastinate? Is it because you think you work better under pressure, so (consciously or not) effectively ensure that you have no choice but to work up to the last minute? If so, it might help to break down the task into chunks and set deadlines for sections of work, rather than producing the whole thing in a rush, which is likely to lead to poor work.

Often, we put off daunting tasks, perhaps through an unconscious fear of failure, so avoiding the issue altogether seems a better option, at least for a while. Perhaps we simply do not know where to start, so we postpone the task in the hope that inspiration will strike or something will happen to make it easier. The job then becomes increasingly intimidating as it gets more urgent – we get trapped in a vicious circle. When we finally make a start, we usually find it is nothing like as difficult as we had built it up to be. The key is to face the challenge and make a start. If you do so early, you can get help along the way.

If you know you tend to procrastinate, you need to make it harder for yourself to avoid the problem than to tackle it – ask a colleague to nag you, or programme your computer to give you irritating reminders, so you have the extra motivation to get them 'off your back'. Sometimes it helps to have a treat or reward in store for completing the work, or even staged mini-rewards for finishing each section.

7. Write out of order if necessary

Word processors mean that we are no longer bound to write documents starting at the beginning and continuing slavishly to the end. If you get stuck on a particular section, move on and come back to it later. Just as some of us read the conclusion of a report first, some people write it first, finding this helps ensure that the statement as a whole works logically towards that reasoned conclusion.

Others prefer to start with the easier sections – personal details, family structure; this can be encouraging as the word count rises quickly. Often it is worth writing something, even if you know it is not perfect. It is better to have something to work on, amend, re-word and get help with than to have everything swimming around in your head.

8. Don't rely too much on computers

Marvellous as they are, computers can also be the source of errors. If you cut and paste, remember to read the paragraphs before and after the moved section to ensure it flows as a whole, and that there is no change of tense, terminology or style from one paragraph to the next. Make sure numbers still follow in the correct order and check that the layout is not disrupted, causing, for example, disembodied headings to appear at the foot of the page.

Sometimes it is tempting to borrow a sentence or paragraph from another report you have written, or perhaps a colleague's statement which you find effective. Make sure this fits with the rest of the statement – a sudden change of style or tone can jar. Students are often amazed that their tutors can spot plagiarism, but if a section of published text is inserted word for word into the student's work, the reader immediately and instinctively feels the abrupt change.

If you copy a paragraph relating to one child into a document about another, check very carefully that it really is appropriate and ensure that the name is changed every single time. In care plans where the plans for siblings are practically identical, it is sometimes apparent that the worker drafted the care plan for the oldest then simply re-hashed it for the younger children. Too often, one child's name slips into a plan supposedly about a different child. This smacks of a lack of care, even a lack of importance accorded to the second child, implying that the children are treated as a 'job lot'. Tempting as it is to save time, consider very carefully whether the words you have used are just as appropriate for one child as for the other.

Spell checks can be helpful, but remember that they sometimes offer American spellings and they cannot spot mistakes which still result in real words, which can entirely change the sense of a sentence. An accidental 'not' which is meant to be a 'now' makes all the difference: 'He is not doing well in foster care.' Remember always to apply your brain as well as the spell check – this did not happen when a letter was sent to Great Hormone Street Hospital.

9. Read, redraft and re-read

When you have finished writing your document, put it aside for a while before re-reading it. If you re-read it straight away, you cannot see it with a fresh eye and will miss mistakes, as you know what it is supposed to say. Make sure that you are happy with every single word of your statement – you have to answer to it in the witness box.

Always print off a copy of your statement rather than just reading it on screen – it is surprising how different things look on the printed page. Is it too long or too short? Is it repetitive? Is it clear?

Re-read your statement several times, considering it from the perspective of the others who will read it. Ask yourself whether your lawyer will be happy that you have covered all the necessary ground. What will the parents and their solicitors pick up on? Where will the child's representatives find fault? Above all, does the statement give the court the information and analysis it needs to make the right decision?

10. Ask someone else to check your statement

It is always useful to have someone else's view of your statement. A colleague in your team but not involved in the case can give a fresh perspective and tell you whether you have explained the situation clearly enough to someone who, like the court, does not know the family.

You need constructive criticism. However nice it might feel, it is no use to you to be told that your work is brilliant – there is always room for improvement. It is far better to be challenged by, and receive helpful suggestions from, someone 'on your side' than to be lulled into a false sense of security only to be put through the mill by the other parties.

Naturally, your lawyer should check your statement before it is submitted. Her workload is probably as heavy as yours, so she needs to receive your statement well before the deadline to review it properly. She reads it from a lawyer's perspective, anticipating likely challenges, and may suggest changes or additions. However, it remains your statement, not the lawyer's, so do not accept any changes you do not agree with.

Email allows drafts to be circulated quickly, but first make sure that there is sufficient security on your system to allow such confidential information to be sent safely and always follow any protocols set by your authority. Statements can be amended on screen and returned to sender but if you do allow someone to do this, be absolutely sure that you know what changes they have made – for example use the track changes facility on your word processing package – or you could be surprised by the contents of your own statement. Ultimately you have to sign a hard copy. Be certain that the copy you sign is the final and approved version with all amendments incorporated and all corrections made. It is surprisingly easy to get this wrong.

Never, ever put your signature to a statement without taking the time to re-read it, line by line.

QUESTIONS FOR REFLECTION

- What are your strengths and weaknesses in writing?
- How can you address the aspects you find difficult?

Chapter 7

Negotiations and Settlements

Negotiations

When we think about court proceedings, we naturally focus on the court itself and the prospect of a trial. In fact, the majority of cases never go to a contested hearing and the whole system is geared towards narrowing the issues between the parties and avoiding conflict wherever possible. The court is no longer a passive recipient of the cases presented to it by the parties; instead it has a duty to manage cases actively to achieve its 'overriding objective' (set out in the Family Procedure Rules 2010[1]), which is to 'deal with cases justly, having regard to any welfare issues involved'. The parties have a duty to help the court to achieve this objective.

'Dealing with cases justly' includes the court acting expeditiously, fairly and proportionately to the nature, importance and complexity of issues in the case. The court is also charged with 'ensuring that the parties are on an equal footing'. However, it can sometimes be difficult for disadvantaged parents to believe that they can fight on equal terms with the full forces of the local authority and partner agencies.

In a sign of the times, the court must also think about saving expense and ensuring an appropriate allocation of resources to the case, bearing in mind all the other demands on limited resources.

The rules list various ways in which a court can actively manage a case.

---

1   Available   at   www.justice.gov.uk/courts/procedure-rules/family/rules_pd_menu, accessed on 11 December 2014.

Family Procedure Rules – meaning of Active Case Management

1.4

(2) Active case management includes: ...

  (c) deciding promptly

    (i) which issues need full investigation and hearing and which do not...

  (g) helping the parties to settle the whole or part of the case

  (h) encouraging the parties to co-operate with each other in the conduct of proceedings

  (i) considering whether the likely benefits of taking a particular step justify the cost of taking it

  (j) dealing with as many aspects of the case as it can on the same occasion

  (k) dealing with the case without the parties needing to attend at court...

Court proceedings do not mean the end of working with the family; instead it is a new phase of negotiations. Even before issuing proceedings, except in an emergency, a last-ditch attempt must be made to avoid them with a pre-proceedings letter and meeting (see Chapter 8).

Once proceedings start, the Guardian, lawyers and the court all become involved in ongoing negotiations through correspondence, phone calls and meetings, including some meetings which are programmed into the court timetable. Negotiations continue right up to the court door.

Social workers often feel uncomfortable about this process; it feels like horse trading, haggling and doing a deal over a child's life. You would not have applied for a care order if you did not think it was the right thing, so why would you change your mind? Remember no one can force you to compromise or accept a settlement against your will. It is open to the local authority to refuse to bend one inch and to urge the court to hear the case in full and make the decision. However, that may not always be the most productive approach.

In fact there are good reasons for negotiations. Sometimes, an original suggestion is made which you have not considered before. In other cases, a way forward is found which was simply not possible previously because one of the other parties had to move first – for example, the child's mother finally admits that all is not rosy and she needs help or maybe that she needs to separate from her violent partner.

Sometimes the right approach for the case changes with time – you might need to try a different service or approach which might work, or if it doesn't, at least you can tell the court you tried. The evidence might just not hold up as you anticipated and you might have to be realistic and settle for half a loaf instead of none. Or a new piece of evidence comes to light which alters your perspective of the case and requires a change of tack. All kinds of developments can affect how the case proceeds and, together with your lawyer, you need to play your hand to achieve the best realistic outcome for the child.

Why cases settle at court

Most care cases reach agreement at least on the threshold criteria well before final hearing. But even now, sometimes a settlement is reached at the very last minute, even on the day of the final hearing. Parents who have been fighting tooth and nail throughout can suddenly cave in when they get to court, or sometimes they simply fail to turn up to the hearing. Why?

- Suddenly it is real – seeing everyone at court, knowing the judge is there, somehow it all becomes too overwhelming.

- Maybe they knew in their heart of hearts all along but could not face reality until they had no choice.

- All the evidence, reports and arguments are now in and there is no more hope of one last report changing everything.

- The idea of all the evidence about their failings being rehearsed in court is just too much to bear.

How do negotiations work?

As we have seen, the court is there to hear only matters which are truly in dispute. The court encourages parties to try to reach agreement on some or all of the issues and, if this happens, the agreement is presented to court for approval. However, it is important to realise that this is not just a rubber stamping exercise and the court can reject a proposed agreement, insisting on hearing the matter instead.

However, if the court is happy that the agreement is a sensible one, the case can be resolved quickly without the need to hear evidence. This makes the hearing much less painful for all concerned as well as saving time and resources. The child gets the order he needs more quickly and can be told that everyone agreed it was the right thing for him.

The question is how to get to that agreed position. One possibility is that the parents simply give in and accept everything you say. However, they also wish to achieve something in these proceedings and there may have to be a little give and take to get to the goal of a sensible agreement. The objective in negotiations is to reach a 'win win' position so everyone can leave court satisfied and with their heads held high. That takes clear thinking and careful planning.

Before entering into any discussions at any stage of the proceedings, you need to know:

- your ideal outcome

- your realistic expected outcome

- the other parties' objectives and likely negotiation points (remembering that there may be several different parties, each with a differing perspective)

- what is negotiable

- what is non-negotiable

- your bottom line, below which you will not go

- how much authority you personally have to compromise the case, when you need to contact your senior, and how to contact her on the day of any meeting or hearing.

This thinking needs to be done in advance and in conjunction with your legal team. If you leave it until the day of a meeting or the hearing itself and all proposals come as a complete surprise, you are unlikely to be able to think sufficiently quickly on your feet and may find yourself railroaded into an agreement which, on reflection, is not the best outcome. Imagine how much pressure you could be under if the parents and Guardian, through their articulate and forceful barristers, put forward a proposal which could save five days of court time and avoid the need for you or anyone else to give evidence. The temptation to agree could be irresistible.

You need to make sure that your lawyer is fully briefed, that he knows the case, understands the issues and has sufficient information about how your department works to ensure that he does not make unrealistic suggestions or commitments during negotiations (such as agreeing to long periods of supervised contact at a family centre without being aware of the resources available – or, more probably, not available). Make sure he understands exactly what he is authorised to propose or to compromise and the limits of his authority. This is particularly important as before critical hearings, advocates' meetings are programmed in to the court timetable. These are compulsory and, as their name suggests, are for advocates (solicitors or barristers) only, so you will not be present to hear or participate in discussions. However, if you are the key social worker, you should be at the end of a phone so the advocate can take your instructions on any developments or proposals made.

However constructive they may be, advocates' meetings are unlikely to resolve everything and further discussions are still likely at court. If you are present during discussions, remember that agreement may not be reached and you may still end up in court, so be careful not to say anything you might regret, or to give away any weaknesses in your case which could be thrown back at you in cross-examination. Neither should you agree to anything without discussing it in private with your lawyer first. If you need to ask any questions, want to make any suggestions or to take advice, withdraw to discuss matters with your lawyer and make sure you are out of earshot of the other parties before you start talking.

What are negotiations about?

Obviously, the precise details of negotiations depend on the details of the case. The strength of each party's bargaining position depends on the evidence, and the position of the Guardian and any experts can be very influential too. Put yourself in the shoes of the parents' advocate. What would you ideally like to achieve? What can you realistically salvage for your client? What can you offer to make a 'deal' more attractive to the local authority? How can you best play your hand?

Scenario: Is an interim care order necessary?

The local authority applies for an interim care order (ICO) in respect of Lottie who is already in foster care. Her mother, Millie, accepts that Lottie should remain in foster care until the final hearing. What does Millie's solicitor want to achieve? He wants to:

- avoid the court hearing too much evidence adverse to his client

- stress that his client is fully co-operative and sensible

- avoid an ICO which would give the local authority the upper hand at an early stage.

Millie's solicitor's ideal is to achieve an adjournment without an ICO. What, then, will he do before court? He will:

- stress that Lottie will remain in foster care, achieving the local authority's main objective without an order

- emphasise Millie's full co-operation

- remind the local authority that there has been no problem with voluntary accommodation and the local authority has been content with that until now

- remind the local authority of the 'no order' principle in the Children Act 1989 and the doctrine of proportionality under the Human Rights Act 1998

- stress that Lottie will be under the protection of the court proceedings throughout – the case can always be brought back to court on short notice if necessary

- remind the local authority that if Millie fails to co-operate, the local authority will have an unanswerable case next time

- imply that the local authority will lose face when it applies for an interim order and is unsuccessful

- offer a written agreement signed by Millie which can be filed at court

- as a fall-back position (it always being wise to have a plan B in case plan A fails), if he cannot avoid a hearing, limit it to submissions on the 'no order' principle and avoid any evidence being heard.

What does the local authority need to be prepared for and to say in response?

Obviously it must be very clear why it wants an ICO in spite of Millie's co-operation and Lottie's accommodation in foster care. If it cannot give a good reason for an order it will win neither the negotiations nor the court application.

A tightly drawn written agreement might be a good solution for all concerned at this stage, provided the local authority is clear exactly what needs to be included in such an agreement, which must be drafted unambiguously. It can then be presented to the court for consideration and, hopefully, approval. The court does not then need to hear any evidence, provided it is happy that Lottie is adequately protected in the interim.

So the social worker and her legal team need to be very clear about the following before even applying for an ICO, bearing in mind that interim orders are by no means inevitable in care proceedings:

- Is an ICO is needed and, if so, precisely why?

- Could a written agreement be enough and, if so, exactly what terms are required?

- Who has the authority to compromise the application – the social worker or a more senior officer?

Scenario: Contact negotiations

Nigella is in foster care under an ICO. Her mother, Odette, unsuccessfully contested the first hearing and nothing has changed since. Odette wants Nigella home. Contact is currently twice a week for 1½ hours at the family centre.

What is Odette's solicitor likely to do?

Since the Children and Families Act 2014 came into force, ICOs can be made for the length of time the court thinks fit, including until the final hearing. Under an ICO, the local authority determines the placement. Unless the court made a time-limited ICO with a view to reviewing the case, there is no realistic prospect of an immediate return home, so Odette's solicitor will advise her to concentrate on securing Nigella's return in the long term and the obvious next step is to seek more contact. The ideal would be a programme of phased increases in contact, leading ultimately to rehabilitation, starting with more and longer visits, building towards trips out, then contact at home and so on. Realistically, the solicitor knows it is unlikely that she will secure the whole programme in one go, so she might settle for some increase at this stage, and (presuming Odette co-operates and does well at contact) seek more next time. If the local authority does not agree, she could seek a hearing for a defined interim contact order.

To be prepared for these discussions, the local authority team of social worker and lawyer need to have information about the contact visits to date, so liaison with contact supervisors and the foster carer is critical. Has Odette attended regularly? What is the quality of contact? How does Nigella react before, during and after contact? Before any step in proceedings, whether or not you expect there to be any controversy, always ensure that you are fully informed about the current situation, having spoken to those directly involved, and make sure that you pass this information on to your lawyer.

In discussions about contact, the worker needs to be able to say why she chose the current level in the first place – who or what is it for? If she cannot explain this, she cannot counter Odette's request for longer or more frequent contact. Courts are usually deeply unimpressed by resource-led answers. 'That's all the family centre could provide' is not a good reason to determine how often Nigella sees her mother. If the family centre is not available more frequently, the riposte is likely to be that there are other possible venues, such as the foster home, Odette's home, an extended family member's home or McDonald's.

Sometimes it can be a good strategy to call someone's bluff. Of course this is out of the question if Odette poses a real danger to Nigella, but sometimes it can be worth going along with the parent's request. If contact is offered, say, five days a week, at different times of day, sometimes early in the morning, sometimes at mealtimes, then Odette's commitment and her relationship with Nigella are really tested out. Either it works, in which case all well and good, or it fails, providing clear evidence for the court. Either way, the local authority shows itself to be accommodating Odette's wishes and trying its best to make things work.

If, on the other hand, contact continues at the current level and is of reasonable quality, the evidence remains unclear. At the final hearing Odette's lawyers can emphasise the positives and argue that contact shows that Nigella can come home. The local authority counters that a couple of sessions of contact a week is very different from full-time care, but this situation is of the authority's own making and the evidence of contact does not demonstrate why Nigella cannot return home.

Sometimes requests are made for a change of social worker – perhaps on grounds of gender (a teenage boy wants a male worker), or racial or cultural origin (a black family wants a black worker) or personality (the family says they do not get on with the particular social worker). There may of course be good reasons why such requests cannot be granted – perhaps no black workers are available, or the child already has a strong relationship with the allocated worker – but it is always worth considering carefully. Changing a worker does not imply acceptance of any criticisms and that can be clearly spelled out. Particularly where the request is made simply because the family dislikes the allocated worker, there seems to be almost a reflex defensive response to deny the request because parents cannot be allowed to dictate who is allocated to a case. It is worth reflecting on this for a moment. We have all met people who, perhaps for no apparent reason at all, we do not warm to. Imagine being expected to discuss the most intimate aspects of your life with such a person – would you not ask for a change of worker, and resent it if your request were denied?

A change of worker sometimes works wonders – a productive relationship is established, progress is achieved. Sometimes the parents characterise the first worker as the 'baddie' and put all their resentment and bitterness about the situation onto her, allowing them to move on and work constructively with someone else.

Other parents are unable to work with anyone and soon complain about the next person. But if a change of worker is tried, by the time of the final hearing the local authority has clear evidence of its good faith and flexibility as well as demonstrating that the problem lies with the parents, not the authority. Inability to co-operate with any professionals in the local authority and other agencies involved in a child's life can be highly significant. In one important Supreme Court decision,[2] the parents' inability to work with professionals was one of

---

2   *Re B (A Child)* [2013] UKSC 33.

the key factors leading to a care order with an adoption plan. As Lord Wilson put it:

> Family Courts regularly make allowance for the negative attitude of parents towards the social workers who personify their employers' applications for care orders. But the level of the dishonest, manipulative, antagonistic obstructionism of the parents in this case was of a different order. Such attributes of course betokened a lack of insight into the needs of Amelia which raised wider concerns; but more immediately, they precluded the success of any rehabilitative programme, whatever its precise composition.

Scenario: Debating the final care plan

Peter is five. By the time of the final hearing the evidence shows that his mother, Queenie, cannot care for him full time. However, Queenie has been committed to contact throughout and everyone agrees that there is a positive relationship between Peter and his mother. Because of his age, and as there is no placement available within the extended family, the local authority plans to place Peter for adoption. It applies for a care order and a placement order, judging a permanent placement to be more important for Peter than continued contact.

Queenie's solicitor has advised her that the local authority's case is strong and it is hopeless to try to contest the care order. It may even be counter-productive to do so, as this would show her as lacking insight, she would have to go through days of hearing demoralising damning evidence and could end up with stronger findings against her than if she concedes the care order. If the care order is a lost cause, what then is her solicitor's approach?

His ideal objective is to secure a change in the care plan, for example, to long-term fostering (possibly with the existing foster carer with whom Peter is obviously thriving) with ongoing contact rather than adoption. He can argue that this would be consistent with the Human Rights Act, specifically Peter and Queenie's rights under Article 8, which makes it clear that any interference with family life must be proportionate. He will argue that adoption (which would terminate all legal relationships between mother and son) would be disproportionate in the circumstances.

He can tell the local authority that his client could accept a care order, saving everyone time and trouble, but in return needs some concessions on contact.

His fall-back position may be to accept adoption as a care plan, but to seek a contact order alongside the placement order.

If he cannot secure a contact order compelling the local authority to place with ongoing contact, he might instead seek a commitment in the care plan to try at least for a specified period to find adopters who accept ongoing contact.

The local authority should already have considered these possibilities in case planning. It should know whether or not the current foster carer could keep Peter long term. Arguments about the respective merits of long-term fostering and adoption as well as other options such as placement with the extended family or of Special Guardianship should all have been rehearsed and resolved long since, as should the issue of post-adoption contact.

The court will not accept a simple proposition that because Peter is only five and cannot go home, adoption is inevitably the best option. Indeed, the Court of Appeal[3] has expressed itself in strident terms about 'the recurrent inadequacy of the analysis and reasoning put forward in support of the case for adoption', saying 'sloppy practice must stop'.[4] You can be quite sure that Queenie's solicitor will have a copy of this case report in his briefcase.

Nor will a court accept that it is impossible to find adopters to accept 'open' adoption; where contact is beneficial for the child, evidence should show that this option has been properly explored before being rejected as impracticable. The court can, of course, make an order for contact against the local authority's wishes even if that effectively means changing the care plan. Evidence of matters such as the likelihood of placement and feasibility of ongoing direct contact in an adoptive placement should be given by the appropriate witness, such as a member of the adoption team rather than the key social worker.

Always beware of the danger of contact being seen as a 'consolation prize' for the parent who is losing a child. Also beware of the temptation to settle to avoid immediate difficulties, only to set up problems for the future.

---

3   *Re B-S (Children)* [2013] EWCA Civ 1146 Munby P at para. 30.
4   *Re B-S* at para. 40.

Scenario: Rehabilitation

Care proceedings are coming to a conclusion with Roger recently placed at home with his father, Sam. Everyone agrees that rehabilitation is the right plan. To date, all looks good and there is a co-operative working relationship between Sam and the social worker.

Everyone is keen to avoid conflict and no one wants the court process to jeopardise the positive situation. Sam's solicitor can use that as a bargaining point to urge the local authority to take the least adversarial line possible.

Sam's solicitor argues:

- The case should be concluded with no order at all. He cites the 'no order' principle in the Children Act and the proportionality principle under the Human Rights Act. He wants to avoid any findings adverse to his client which may have implications for the future, not just for Roger but for any future children.

- In the past, he could have argued for an adjournment to test the placement for a while with proceedings continuing. However, this has become a harder case to make with the advent of the 26-week statutory limit on care proceedings.[5] The timescale can only be extended is if the court considers that the extension necessary to enable it to resolve the proceedings justly. At the time of writing, we are in the early days of the new provision and time will tell whether a case such as Roger's is strong enough to meet this strict test.

- As a fall-back position, he could argue for a supervision order, rather than a care order, relying on a string of case law authorities which indicate that where a child is placed at home the presumption is in favour of the least Draconian order, namely a supervision order.

---

5   Introduced by s14 Children and Families Act 2014, which amends s32 Children Act 1989.

The local authority should be very clear what order, if any, is required, when and why. It may decide to support an application for an extension of the proceedings. But if the case has to be concluded before rehabilitation is sufficiently tried and tested, the authority may feel that a care order is the only safe proposal. However, there are disadvantages in having a care order over a child placed at home – the local authority would have legal responsibility for Roger, but little actual control. If the rehabilitation works, another court case would later be required to discharge the care order. If the rehabilitation proves unsuccessful, it might still be necessary to return to court for another order such as a placement order, if adoption is the contingency plan, or an order regulating contact. From the authority's managers' point of view, statistics are another consideration – why have another child under a care order if it is not necessary? The case requires a clear-headed analysis of the legal implications of each option weighed up against Roger's needs.

Scenario: Agreeing the threshold findings

Care proceedings are underway in respect of Tim and Ursula's children. The local authority seek care orders and orders giving leave to refuse contact under s34(4) Children Act 1989, the plan being long-term fostering. The local authority's case rests on three main issues:

1. Sexual abuse of the children by Tim, the evidence being the children's disclosures and medical signs 'consistent' with sexual abuse, although Tim was acquitted in the criminal court.

2. Physical abuse in the form of excessive chastisement including beating the children with a stick.

3. Emotional abuse, especially both parents' emotional rejection of the children.

Up to the final hearing, the parents contest all three points, strenuously denying sexual abuse, claiming that their punishment of the children was reasonable and consistent with their religious faith, and rejecting allegations of emotional abuse. However, although they deny the allegations, they do not want the children back or to see them again, so hurt and betrayed do they feel

This means that their solicitor can tell the local authority it can have the orders it wants, the witnesses can all go home and everyone can breathe a sigh of relief. What else is there left to argue about?

But it is not just a question of orders. The local authority must also consider the findings on which they are based – the court can only make a care order if the s31 threshold criteria are met. Negotiations in this case therefore turn on whether the findings can be agreed. The temptation to reach agreement is very strong, but in an effort to compromise, the local authority and the court must not allow the findings to be watered down too far. Many of us have seen agreed findings which barely cross the threshold and are so understated as to be nearly meaningless – another example of the 'sloppy practice' the Court of Appeal spoke of.

Tim and Ursula accept that they have hit the children, although they believe they had Biblical authority for this and do not accept that it was inappropriate. They admit that they have now emotionally rejected the children, but they say that this is the children's fault because of their false allegations. They are willing to accept a threshold document recording these concessions. They are absolutely not prepared to sign up to anything mentioning sexual abuse.

Can the local authority accept Tim and Ursula's offer? The local authority team needs to consider the strength or otherwise of the evidence and consider the longer-term consequences of findings. What if, a couple of years on, Tim and Ursula ask to see the children or if they have another child? The social worker at that time will no doubt look at the court's findings. She might take a very different decision depending on how those findings were worded, including whether or not there are findings of sexual abuse.

There are implications for the children themselves, including questions of therapy and criminal injuries compensation. The local authority might just have to bite the bullet and insist on the court hearing evidence even though the orders themselves are conceded. Even if the local authority does not do so, the court could insist, refusing to accept a watered-down agreement. There may be a desire to work in a non-adversarial way wherever possible, but the bottom line is that the court is there to 'deal with the case justly'. Sometimes reaching agreement is not the right thing to do.

Scenario: Threshold concessions

Vanessa's case also turns on the issue of findings. She is an 18-year old mother who had a difficult childhood herself and, although she tried to look after baby William, accepts she could not manage. She agrees to a care order and placement order, with a view to William's adoption.

What, then, can Vanessa's solicitor achieve for her?

The best he can realistically hope for is:

- the best assurances he can achieve about ongoing contact (indirect at least)

- input for his client in the adoption process (choice of adopters, meeting adopters, preparing life book/letter/gift)

- mildly worded agreed findings which will do as little damage as possible to Vanessa's prospects of keeping any babies she may have in the future

- positive comments from the judge about how brave Vanessa is in reaching this difficult decision, putting her child's interests above her own.

Judges often, quite rightly, pay tribute to parents in cases where they concede orders, enabling them to leave court with some dignity even after losing their child. Imagine the contrast to the damning judgment describing every last failure which might have followed a contested hearing in the same case.

This is one of the reasons why parents' solicitors must be plain-speaking, sometimes brutally honest with their clients about their prospects of success should they choose to contest. Imagine how it feels to spend days in court having your life dissected and your every move criticised by one witness after another, followed by a judgment detailing your failings as a parent, on top of the pain of losing your child. Sometimes, therefore, the best service a parent's solicitor can give to his client is to help her recognise reality and to end the proceedings with some self-esteem intact.

Conclusion

Negotiations are an integral part of court proceedings. Be prepared for them. Be clear about your objectives and realistic about your prospects. Be open to suggestions or new ways of thinking, always putting the child's best interests at the heart of your deliberations. Always work closely with your legal team.

QUESTIONS FOR REFLECTION

- How can you ensure that in every case you are systematically ready for negotiations and have anticipated the likely areas for discussion?

- How can you ensure that your legal team is sufficiently well briefed on the nuances of the case and your department's procedures and resources in order to negotiate effectively on your behalf?

Chapter 8

Procedure – The Public Law Outline and Experts

The PLO

Procedure can be dry and frustrating. Form filling and administration can seem far from your focus on the welfare of the child. However, understanding the process and complying with the court's requirements is crucial to achieving the right outcome for the child. Failure to follow procedures correctly could undermine your own professional reputation along with that of your local authority. It could even impede your ability to achieve the right result for the child.

Radical changes have recently been introduced in an effort to bring under control proceedings which had grown out of all proportion. The process itself was doing a disservice to the very children who were supposed to be at the heart of the system, with care proceedings regularly taking over a year to resolve. That is no longer acceptable.

There is now a statutory 26-week time limit[1] on care proceedings. As The President of the Family Division, Sir James Munby P, said:[2]

> My message is clear and uncompromising: this deadline can be met, it must be met, it will be met. And remember, 26 weeks is a deadline, not a target; it is a maximum, not an average or a mean. So many cases will need to be finished in less than 26 weeks.

Courts now have greater case management powers and are expected to take active control of cases before them.

---

1   s32 Children Act 1989 as amended by s14 Children and Families Act 2014.
2   'The View from the President's Chambers – The process of reform' [2013], p.4, available at www.judiciary.gov.uk/publications/view-from-presidents-chambers/, accessed on 3 September, 2014.

Of course sometimes, despite the best efforts of all involved, 26 weeks will not be enough to do justice to the case and make the right decision for the child. As Pauffley J said,[3] 'Justice must never be sacrificed upon the altar of speed.' So in such cases, an extension of time is possible, but such cases are very much the exception, not the norm.

The details of procedure are set out in the Family Procedure Rules 2010 Practice Direction 12A.[4] The key stages in the court process are prescribed in the Public Law Outline, universally known as 'the PLO'. The flow chart setting out the stages in proceedings is reproduced in Appendix 4.

Before proceedings

Except in emergencies, steps must be taken before starting proceedings in a last-ditch attempt to avoid having to go to court at all, and to be absolutely sure that the parents are in no doubt about the seriousness of the situation. It is also important to consider involving the wider family, perhaps by holding a family group conference before it is too late.

Legal planning meeting

A meeting with your legal team is essential to:

- take legal advice on the threshold criteria (the grounds for care proceedings) (see Appendix 1)

- assess what evidence exists

- decide what further evidence or assessments are needed

- discuss the likely care plan for the child

- determine whether to start proceedings and, if so, when.

You know the parents better than anyone else in the case. If you are aware of any issue which might impact on a parent's capacity to take part in proceedings (such as mental health problems, learning

---

3   *Re NL (A child) (Appeal: Interim Care Order: Facts and Reasons)* [2014] EWHC 270 (Fam).
4   Available at www.justice.gov.uk/courts/procedure-rules/family/practice_directions/ pd_part_12a, accessed on 26 August 2014.

disabilities or communication difficulties such as problems with reading and writing, or the need for an interpreter), raise them immediately. Human Rights legislation demands that the whole process must be fair, so steps must be taken to make sure that disadvantaged parties can participate throughout the process. If you think there is an issue at any stage, even if no one else involved does, make sure you raise the issue – expert advice may be necessary or other directions made to ensure that the process is fair.

Letter before proceedings

If immediate action is required, of course you should go ahead and issue proceedings first and then inform the parties immediately thereafter, by sending a 'letter of issue'.

In less urgent cases, the local authority must send to everyone with PR a 'letter before proceedings', setting out in straightforward terms that the matter is likely to go to court. To be absolutely sure that this arrives safely, it should be delivered by hand or sent by recorded delivery. In due course, the court will want proof that the parents received the letter.

Department for Education statutory guidance[5] provides a standard template which can be adapted to the particular case. It is reproduced in Appendix 3.

The letter must set out unambiguously and in plain English:

- the fact that concerns are very serious

- there is one last chance to avoid proceedings

- an outline of the main concerns

- the date, time and place of the pre-proceedings meeting

- the right to free legal advice

- advice to the parents to involve their wider family.

---

5   Court orders and pre-proceedings for local authorities issued by the Department for Education April 2014 are available at www.justice.gov.uk/protecting-the-vulnerable/care-proceedings-reform, accessed on 26 August 2014. This guidance is issued under s7 Local Authority Social Services Act 1970 so must be followed unless there is a very good reason to make an exception.

Examples of concerns

Neglect

You do not feed Ben properly. He is seriously overweight. This is already badly affecting his health and if things do not change it will be very harmful for him as he grows up. He is not able to run and play like other children and he is unhappy. He is teased at school and does not want to go to school any more. This damages his education and his chances in life.

Domestic violence

Your relationship is violent. The children have seen and heard you shouting at each other, hitting each other and being abusive to each other. This has a serious emotional effect on the children, who are frightened, unhappy and stressed. We believe that Jack wets the bed because he is upset by your rows.

Sexualised behaviour

Tammy behaves in a very sexualised way. At school she has rubbed a male teacher's crotch, has fondled other children and pulled down her knickers to display her private parts. She has asked other children to 'sex' her. This behaviour is not normal for a child of her age.

Pre-proceedings meeting

As is clear from the letter, the next step is a meeting between the local authority and the parents (and others with PR). Parents are entitled to non-means-tested Legal Aid for this meeting, so they should have legal advice, perhaps for the first time. This in itself can help to move things forward even in apparently intractable cases.

The meeting is a final attempt to address concerns without going to court, so the local authority should spell out clearly and precisely:

- what needs to change

- the timescales for improvement or action, and

- the support to be provided.

The meeting should also look at any alternative care which might be available in the wider family. Failure to consider this issue at an early stage has often led to delay for children later on.

If matters fail to improve within the prescribed timetable, the authority has no alternative but to apply to court. It is good practice to inform CAFCASS or CAFCASS Cymru once the decision has been made to launch proceedings.

Court application

There is a long list of documents to be prepared and submitted to court with a care proceedings application. Of course, in an urgent case, the lack of documentation must not hold up necessary action, so if particular information is not available, you can explain why and provide it as soon as possible thereafter.

Application form

The 22-page application form C110A[6] must be completed and signed. The original plus four copies, all of the supporting documents and the fee (£2055 at the time of writing) must be taken to the Family Court for issue. You should send a copy to CAFCASS/CAFCASS Cymru at the same time.

The same form is used for care proceedings or an Emergency Protection Order and a single form covers all the children of the same family.

It takes time, care and a lot of detail to complete the form but it is clearly set out, relatively straightforward and very comprehensive.

The information includes:

THE PARTIES

- Name of the applicant local authority and respondents (including those with PR and the child himself), and their full details including their relationship to each of the children (bearing in mind that the children in the family might have different fathers, for example).

---

6   Available at www.justice.gov.uk/protecting-the-vulnerable/care-proceedings-reform, accessed on 26 August 2014.

- Anyone else who should be given notice of the proceedings (such as fathers without PR or people who the child was living with).

Parties to proceedings

Anne has three children – Beth aged 13, Charlie aged 6 and Damien aged 8 months. Anne and the children are automatically respondents. Given her age, Beth may well be able to give her own instructions to her solicitor. All three children will have a Children's Guardian to represent their interests.

Beth's father is Ed. He does not have PR for Beth so he is not a party, but he receives notice of the proceedings so he can apply to take part if he wants.

Charlie's father, Fred, was married to Anne. He has PR so is a respondent.

Damien's father is unknown. Enquiries will have to be made of Anne, to try to identify who he is.

Anne's current partner is Gerry, who has been living with Anne and the children for the last year, so although he is not a party, he receives notice of the proceedings.

THE APPLICATION

The form must specify:

- The nature of the application (care order, supervision order or emergency protection order [EPO]) including:

    ○ any interim orders sought (ICO or interim supervision order [ISO]); and

    ○ in care proceedings, whether adoption is under consideration and if so, whether and when a placement order application will be made.

- Whether an urgent hearing or (in the case of an EPO application) a hearing without notice is needed.

SPECIAL CONSIDERATIONS

- Any issues affecting a party's capacity to litigate, such as mental ill-health or learning difficulties. The court must consider at an early stage whether particular directions are needed, such as inviting the OS to represent a party who is incapable of giving instructions for himself.

- Whether an interpreter or intermediary will be needed.

- Any special arrangements to be made for any of the parties (this could include, for example, the need to keep the parents apart at court in domestic violence cases).

Special Arrangements

Anne's mental ill-health forms part of the concerns for the children. Mental illness does not, of itself, mean that a person is incapable of participating fully in proceedings – it is a question of degree. If Anne is so ill that she cannot comprehend the issues or give instructions to her solicitor, the court will consider whether she needs the OS to represent her interests. A psychiatric report will be needed. The OS's involvement will have to be kept under review as, if Anne's mental health improves part way through the case, the OS may no longer be needed. If the OS is not required, consideration must be given to what other measures need to be taken to ensure that Anne can participate fully in the case.

Fred is deaf. He lip reads and also uses sign language. A sign language interpreter must be instructed, and consideration given to the layout of the courtroom and positioning of the parties to enable Fred to see people so he can lip read.[7]

---

7   For an interesting analysis of the impact of a parent's deafness on proceedings and measures to ensure that proper allowances are made for a parent's disability in care proceedings *see* the Court of Appeal case of *Re C (A Child)* [2014] EWCA Civ 128.

THE CHILD(REN)

- Full details of the children including full names, dates of birth, names of the parents and whether the father has PR, whether the child is voluntarily accommodated in foster care.

PROCEDURAL CONSIDERATIONS

- Whether an early hearing is needed; for example, for a contested ICO.

- Whether there are any previous or ongoing court proceedings so that information can be married up appropriately and continuity preserved; for example, appointing the same Guardian.

THE GROUNDS FOR THE CASE AND PLANS

- The grounds for the proceedings, summarising in no more than two pages why and how the local authority says that the threshold criteria are met (this is of course a highly significant section).

- Plans for the children.

- The timetable for each child, including significant steps anticipated in the child's life during the course of proceedings, such as a change of school or change of placement.

- The authority's view on the appropriate allocation of the case according to its complexity (lay judges, District Judge, Circuit Judge or High Court Judge).

This section is of course the most important and takes the most thought, time and effort to prepare. As Black LJ said,[8] there must be 'active thought from the outset about what the factual and evidential basis of a local authority's case is'. She stressed:

> the need rigorously to confine social work chronologies and statements and the threshold statement, avoiding all unnecessary detail. We must expect threshold statements which no longer get bogged down in the detail of what occurred on this or that particular day or recite the contents of material from the bundle but instead expose the essential

---

8   *P (A Child)* [2013] EWCA Civ 963.

nature of the problems which have led the local authority to consider that intervention into the family's life should be contemplated. This will require social workers and lawyers to adjust their approach. Care cases involve 'professional evaluation, assessment, analysis and opinion' brought to bear on facts.

It is clear that, from the very start, you and your legal team must be rigorous in your thinking, focusing on:

- the statutory basis for your action

- the factual evidence

- your professional analysis of the evidence

- your consequential recommendation.

Supporting documents

The is a substantial list of documents to be provided, and the application form includes a checklist to make sure that nothing has been forgotten. As far as possible, all the documentation should be provided at the outset of the case.

We often talk about 'filing' and 'serving' documents in court cases. To 'file' a document means to provide a copy to the court, and to 'serve' a document means to provide it to the other parties.

Annex documents

The following must be filed at court along with the application form (see Chapters 4 and 5):

- social work chronology

- social work statement

- genogram

- current assessments relating to the child and/or family referred to in the social work statement

- care plan

- index of Checklist documents (these are not copied to the court but the court needs to know what they are).

Checklist documents

If you have any of the following already in your file, they must be served on the other parties (but not filed at court):

- any previous court orders relating to the child

- any previous reports filed at court by the local authority and any assessment materials relevant to questions such as a party's capacity to take part in the proceedings

- any joint or inter-agency materials such as health and education documents.

There are some further documents which you must disclose on request from any party:

- records of key discussions with the family

- key minutes and records

- pre-existing care plans

- the letter before proceedings.

Issuing proceedings
Stage 1 – issue and allocation

Once the court receives all the relevant papers, the court officer issues the application. This is Day 1.

The court takes control of the management of the case. The standard steps are set out in the PLO, but the court has flexible powers and can adapt procedures to suit the case. So it can give directions without a hearing, or take a step at a different stage in the case than specified in the PLO, or it can cancel or repeat a particular hearing. Courts are now expected to take active steps to keep the proceedings moving. Care proceedings must be completed without delay, and in any event within 26 weeks, and the court must always consider the child's welfare when drawing up a timetable.

Which level of judge?

If a case is an emergency – such as an application for an EPO without notice – it can be heard by whichever judge of the Family Court is available, possibly a single lay judge.

In other cases, the court allocates the case to the appropriate level of Family Judge on Day 2. The factors include:

- the need to make the most effective and efficient use of the local judicial resources that is appropriate, given the nature and type of application

- the need to avoid delay

- the need for judicial continuity

- the location of the parties or of any child relevant to the proceedings, and

- the complexity.

Judicial allocation

The concerns for baby Nathan centre on neglect of his basic needs for regular feeds, nappy changing, adequate clothing and emotional care. His case is perfectly suited to lay judges.

Ollie's mother has mental health problems. A report from her psychiatrist will form part of the evidence. Her mental health fluctuates; at times, she reaches the level at which she needs the OS, although currently that is not the case. Ollie's case is appropriate for a Circuit Judge.

Petra has suffered a subdural haematoma with retinal haemorrhaging. The local paediatricians believe it to be a case of shaken baby syndrome. Her parents have no explanation for the injuries and have said they want an expert second opinion. Head injuries are notoriously complex, and the case will probably be allocated to a High Court Judge.

The court gives standard directions including:

- Appointing a Children's Guardian.

- Directing filing and serving by specified dates of:
  - a case summary by the local authority
  - a case analysis by the Guardian to include consideration of:
    - threshold
    - case management including the timetable
    - parenting capability
    - child's welfare and ascertainable wishes and feelings
    - permanence analysis
    - any proposed communication between the child and the court.
  - a 2-page response by the parents including:
    - a response to the threshold statement
    - the parents' placement proposals
    - any information about their capacity to litigate.
  - any application for a permission to instruct an expert.
- Fixing the Case Management Hearing (CMH).
- If an urgent hearing is needed (for example, for a contested ICO), this is listed and necessary directions are given.

The local authority serves on the other parties the application form and supporting documents together with the notice of the CMH and any urgent hearing. Parents and children are entitled to non-means tested Legal Aid so they have legal representation throughout the care proceedings.

Complying with directions

Be in no doubt: directions are court orders which must be complied with to the letter and on time. The President of the Family Division is very clear that non-compliance is a serious matter, especially when the defaulter is a public body. As he put it:[9]

9   *W (A Child); Re H (Children)* [2013] EWCA Civ 1177.

The court is entitled to expect – and from now on Family Courts will demand – strict compliance with all such orders. Non-compliance with orders should be expected to have and will usually have a consequence. Let me spell it out. An order that something is to be done by 4 pm on Friday, is an order to do that thing by 4 pm on Friday, not by 4.21 pm on Friday let alone by 3.01 pm the following Monday or sometime later the following week. A person who finds himself unable to comply timeously with his obligations under an order should apply for an extension of time before the time for compliance has expired. It is simply not acceptable to put forward as an explanation for non-compliance with an order the burden of other work. If the time allowed for compliance with an order turns out to be inadequate the remedy is either to apply to the court for an extension of time or to pass the task to someone else who has available the time in which to do it.

Always make sure you are clear exactly what you need to do and the timescale for doing it. Respect court deadlines.

QUESTION FOR REFLECTION

- How can you make sure that all of your authority's evidence is filed on time?

Stage 2 – Case Management Hearing

The CMH takes place between day 12 and day 18 (day means business day).

At least two days before this hearing there must be an advocates' meeting, organised by the child's solicitor. As the name suggests, it is for advocates only so you will not be present; however, you need to ensure that your advocate is fully briefed in advance, has your contact number available to take instructions on the day if necessary, and informs you immediately of the outcome.

The idea of the meeting is to make the best use of court time by identifying:

- the parties' positions, to be recited in the draft Case Management Order

- any proposed experts (if necessary) and the questions to be asked of them

- any disclosure needed (this may include information from other agencies such as health or the police)

- the need for any contested ICO hearing

- any issue about allocation.

The local authority's advocate files a draft Case Management Order the day before the CMH.

The CMH itself is a procedural hearing which you should attend. The court does not hear evidence, it hears submissions from the advocates, then it gives detailed directions for the case, making sure that everything is considered including:

- Drawing up a timetable for the proceedings and for the child.

- Identifying any additional parties or intervenors and any issues of representation.

- Making any necessary directions for special measures to help vulnerable witnesses give their evidence, or for interpreters or intermediaries. Considerations may include the best court venue for a hearing; for example, some courts have better facilities than others for people with disabilities or better equipment if someone needs to give evidence by video link.

- Identifying the key issues and the evidence required.

- Deciding whether there is a real dispute about the threshold criteria.

- Giving directions for any concurrent placement order application.

- Deciding whether there is a need for expert evidence.

- Making directions for documents to be filed including final evidence, care plan, and case analysis.

- Fixing an Issues Resolution Hearing (IRH) and final hearing.

As the case is timetabled right through to a final hearing at this very early stage, you need to have any necessary information with you about your availability together with that of any key witnesses. Cultural considerations need to be taken into account too, such as bearing in mind holy days on which particular participants may be unavailable. Be prepared to raise such issues even if no one else thinks of them.

Matters for directions

Rosie's case centres on neglect by her parents, but also includes an allegation of sexual abuse against Stuart, a family friend. The local authority seeks a finding that Stuart abused Rosie. Stuart is not a party to the proceedings, nor should he see all the evidence or be involved in every aspect of the case. However, he has a right to defend himself against the allegations, so he can be joined as an intervenor. Directions can be given for him to see the relevant parts of the evidence and for his involvement in only those parts of the hearing as are necessary.

Tomas has suffered multiple bruising. The local authority is so concerned about the risk to him that it is not prepared to leave him at home during the proceedings. It seeks an ICO. The parents oppose, so the matter must be listed for an urgent contested hearing, even before the CMH.

Uri is two years old. The local authority's case is that his parents cannot care for him, nor is there anyone suitable in the extended family. The care plan is for adoption. The sooner the authority can apply for a placement order, the better – the ideal is to timetable both the care and placement applications to be heard at the same time.

Valda's paternity is in dispute. Directions are needed to resolve this at an early stage of the proceedings.

Will's case involves allegations of sexual abuse and there are parallel criminal and care proceedings. Directions are needed to co-ordinate the two sets of proceedings, including appropriate disclosure of information from one case to the other.

Stage 3 – Issues Resolution Hearing

No less than seven days before the IRH, there must be another advocates' meeting to:

- Review the evidence and the parties' positions.

- Identify:

  ○ the remaining key issues and how they can be resolved or narrowed

  ○ further evidence required

  ○ the need for a contested hearing

  ○ the witnesses needed for a final hearing.

The local authority's advocate must tell the court of the outcome of the meeting immediately and file a draft Case Management Order by the morning before the IRH.

At the IRH itself, the court tries to resolve or at least narrow as many issues as possible and can actually use the IRH as a final hearing, including hearing evidence if necessary, so you need to be prepared for this possibility.

Assuming the case cannot be finished at the IRH, the court:

- Identifies the remaining key issues.

- Identifies the evidence to be heard at the final hearing.

- Gives final case management directions including filing:

  ○ the threshold agreement or statement of facts and issues to be determined

  ○ final evidence and care plan

  ○ case analysis for final hearing

  ○ witness templates (setting out who will come to court to give evidence, when and how long each witness is expected to take)

  ○ skeleton arguments (including the parties' legal submissions).

- Gives directions for court bundles to be prepared (the indexed and paginated bundle contains all of the documents filed in the proceedings).

- Lists the final hearing.

Final hearing

This must take place within 26 weeks of issue of the proceedings, other than in exceptional circumstances.

The majority of cases conclude without a contested final hearing. In other cases, only limited issues remain to be heard; for example, agreement is reached on the threshold criteria, so argument is limited to what orders, if any, should be made.

However, for a minority of cases, the court has to hear and decide a contested case. This is the culmination of all the effort and paperwork. By this stage, the court bundle probably stretches over several hundred pages of statements and reports, all of which have been read and absorbed in advance by the parties and the court.

How a contested hearing works

The parties, including the key social worker and their advocates, usually enter court before the judge and remain in court throughout the hearing. Other witnesses are excluded until it is their turn to give evidence.

Everyone rises when the judge or magistrates enters the room. The advocates bow – technically not to the judge, but to the Royal Crest behind his seat. Once the judge is seated, everyone else can sit.

The local authority advocate opens the case. In family cases, as all the information is disclosed in advance, the opening is usually limited to identifying the people in court, briefly outlining the matters in dispute, telling the judge which witnesses he will hear and in what order, and very little else. The hearing moves very quickly to the witnesses' evidence.

As the applicant, the local authority presents its case first, calling its witnesses one after the other in a logical order, but aiming to start and finish with strong witnesses. The key worker in the case is likely to be called first, followed by the other local authority witnesses. However some witnesses, particularly experts, may be called out of turn if they have only limited availability, and all experts in the same field should be heard on the same day.

Oath or affirmation

Each witness starts by taking the oath or affirmation. These promises to tell the truth are of equal value, the only difference being that the oath has a religious basis, whereas the affirmation does not. They signal the formal start of evidence, and anything untrue said thereafter could give rise to a perjury charge. It is a significant moment and everyone else in court should remain silent while the oath is taken. Remember this when you are present when someone else takes the oath.

A witness who elects to take the oath is asked to take the New Testament or other appropriate religious book in her right hand and to read aloud the words on the card held up by the court usher. If you know that a witness cannot read, it is thoughtful to tip the usher off in advance so she can ask that witness to repeat the words after her, rather than read them from the card – it saves embarrassment for all concerned.

The Christian oath and the affirmation

The oath (Christian form): 'I swear by Almighty God that the evidence I shall give shall be the truth, the whole truth and nothing but the truth.'

The affirmation: 'I solemnly, sincerely and truly declare and affirm that the evidence I shall give shall be the truth, the whole truth and nothing but the truth.'

Examination in chief

After the oath comes the witness's 'evidence in chief' when she responds to questions from her own advocate. He is only allowed to ask open questions and cannot lead his own witness. In care proceedings there is no need to go through every single item in a witness's statement. Instead, the witness confirms on oath that the contents of all her statements are true to the best of her knowledge and belief, and this has the same effect as if she had recounted every detail on oath. If there are any errors in her statements, this is the time for her to correct them.

Examination in chief is usually over very quickly.

Cross-examination

Each of the other parties' advocates then questions the witness in turn, with the child's representative always going last. The witness therefore has to answer questions from a number of different advocates, each of whom has a different agenda. Advocates can and invariably do use leading questions in cross-examination. This is usually the lengthiest and most challenging part of being a witness and is considered in more detail in Chapter 11.

Re-examination

The final stage of questioning for each witness is 're-examination' by the advocate who called the witness in the first place. The advocate is not allowed to raise new matters or ask questions he forgot earlier – he can only ask about matters raised in cross-examination, to clarify anything left unclear or to repair any damage done. Re-examination is usually very short.

Judge's questions

Judges can ask any questions they like, whenever they like. Some judges are very interventionist, others say nothing at all – it depends on personal style. Lay judges (magistrates) tend to intervene less than other judges, and usually wait until all the advocates have finished before asking any questions.

Occasionally, even though they automatically receive Legal Aid, parents appear in court without legal representation (often because they have sacked their lawyers). In such cases, the judge may ask more questions of the witnesses to ensure that all the relevant questions have been asked. It may feel like he is taking the parents' side; in fact, he is just ensuring that there is a fair trial and that justice is seen to be done.

When everyone has finished their questions to each witness, the judge gives the witness permission either to resume her seat and listen to the rest of the evidence or to leave the court building.

Respondents' case

Each local authority witness goes through the same process in turn. When they have all given evidence, the local authority's case is concluded and the other parties present their cases, each calling their witnesses. The child's case always goes last, so the final witness is usually the Guardian.

Submissions

When all the evidence is concluded, the advocates make their submissions. Legal arguments have already been put in writing, but are supplemented by oral submissions. Each advocate highlights all the evidence in his client's favour while explaining away adverse evidence, and puts his arguments on relevant statute and case law. Again, the child's case is put last.

Judgment

All that is left then is the judgment, in which the court gives its decision, findings and reasons. Lay judges always give written reasons, so they inevitably have to adjourn to take time to compose the reasons for their decision. District, Circuit and High Court Judges do not have to produce written reasons and usually they give judgment orally in court. In a straightforward case, this may be done immediately after the conclusion of the proceedings. Alternatively, they may decide to adjourn to take time to compose their judgment (in which case consideration must be given to any orders required to preserve the status quo in the meantime). Parties can request a transcript of the judgment. You should always make sure you have a written copy of the judgment so you can study it carefully for the particular case and to learn lessons for future cases. Judges often make comments on the witnesses they heard – who was impressive, who was not. The following chapters should help you to be one of the impressive witnesses.

Expert evidence

Sometimes, in order to make the right decision, the court needs evidence from an expert in a particular field, often a medical discipline, from paediatric radiology to adult psychiatry. When we talk about an expert witness, we generally mean a person who has had no previous involvement with the case, but who is called in specifically for the proceedings. Of course other witnesses working with the family, such as social workers, are also experts and can also give opinion evidence.

> ### Request for expert evidence
>
> Jayden is subject to care proceedings because of multiple bruising found on his body. The local paediatrician who treated him will be a witness in the case and is of course an expert in her own right. Jayden's parents claim that he has a rare blood disorder which causes unexplained bruising. They want to instruct an expert haematologist to give a specialist opinion, along with a consultant paediatrician to review Jayden's notes and examine him.

However much the parties may want to instruct an expert to provide a report for use in care proceedings, or to examine or assess the child, they cannot do so without court leave. Of course, even if the court gives permission, a competent child can refuse to be assessed or examined. The application to court should be made as soon as possible, and certainly by the CMH. This should indicate:

- the precise field of expertise

- if possible, the name of the proposed expert

- the precise questions to be addressed.

The court only gives permission if the expert evidence is necessary to assist the court to resolve the proceedings justly.[10] It is a strict test. 'Necessary' is a strong word – more than simply helpful or desirable. Sometimes there is no simple answer and no expert in the world can give you one. The fact that a party wants their own expert to counter another party's evidence is not enough. A parent facing losing her child does not have an automatic right to an assessment carried out by someone other than the local authority. As Black LJ said,[11]

---

10   s13 Children and Families Act 2014.
11   *Re S* [2011] EWCA Civ 812 (Court of Appeal) at para. 93.

'sadly there are some cases in which the parents are plainly not able to care for their children and in which no amount of assessment or evidence gathering will enable them to put forward a positive case.'

The court will also consider whether the evidence could be given by anyone else already involved in the case, so independent social work evidence is only justified if neither the local authority worker nor the Guardian can help the court. The impact on the timetable and duration of the case is another important consideration.

The need for expert evidence

In Jayden's case, the court agrees that a haematologist's report is necessary to help it to understand the case – the local paediatrician is not sufficiently specialist to be able to give evidence on blood disorders. So in principle the application for a haematologist's report is likely to succeed. However, the application for a second paediatrician is a different matter. There is already a consultant paediatrician in the case. There is no reason to believe that a second expert from the same field is required and this application is likely to be refused.

If you think an expert is needed in your case, raise the issue as soon as possible and be prepared to justify it. Think through exactly what you want to ask the expert – questions need to be clear, focused and manageable in number.

If another party proposes an expert, analyse whether you agree it is necessary, who is suggested and why – you are not bound to accept it, and if you feel it is unnecessary or inappropriate, or that the wrong expert is being suggested, you should instruct your legal team to oppose the application.

You should be fully involved in deciding which expert should be selected. Ask to see a full CV – it is not just a question of qualification in a specific discipline, but specialisation within that field. For example, you may agree that a child psychiatrist is needed, but it is no use instructing a child psychiatrist who specialises in attention deficit hyperactive disorder (ADHD) if the case concerns a teenage girl with anorexia. After considerable concerns about the standard of expert witnesses in court, requirements have now been imposed.[12] For example an expert must:

- have appropriate competence and relevant experience

- have been active in the area of work or practice and be familiar with the current breadth of opinion in the field

- have working knowledge of the relevant social, developmental, cultural norms and accepted legal principles and possess cultural competence skills

- have a current licence to practice or registration and up-to-date continuing professional development and/or supervision (as appropriate to the profession)

- comply with any necessary safeguarding requirements, information security expectations, and carry professional indemnity insurance

- have training in the role of expert and seek feedback from cases

- have a working knowledge of and comply with the relevant Practice Directions.

The statement of truth in an expert's report includes a confirmation that he has complied with all the relevant requirements.

What is the expert's reputation? Do you know anyone who has seen his work – are his reports good and is he effective in court? Some experts are fine on paper, but unimpressive giving oral evidence. How does he conduct his assessments – does he expect the family to go to his consulting rooms in Harley Street or does he come to them? How many sessions of what length does he propose? Be assertive in seeking information to help you decide on the right response to the application.

Other factors such as gender are relevant – a male psychiatrist, however eminent, may not be the right person to assess a sexually abused teenage girl. Racial and cultural issues may also be important, and personality can be a factor. One psychiatrist may have been highly respected but he was blunt to the point of cruelty, including in his report a description of a teenager who may indeed have been overweight and spotty but who did not need to read that in a report.

---

12   Practice Direction 25B plus Annex.

Last but not least, it is of course crucial that the proposed expert can do the work and provide the report in an appropriate timescale.

If two or more parties want experts, they must consider whether a single joint expert could be instructed. The court can order a joint expert even if the parties do not agree, and it can even choose the expert to be instructed.

Who pays?

Naturally expert witnesses do not come cheap; four-figure sums are the norm. The court decides who pays for the report, and unless the expert is specifically concerned with only one party, often the cost is shared between the parties, regardless of who raised the suggestion. Parents and children's solicitors have to secure funding from the Legal Services Commission (LSC). Recently the LSC was successfully judicially reviewed[13] for refusing to pay the costs of an expert psychotherapist, as it had been ordered to do by the court. The local authority also has to find the money somewhere in its budget – no mean feat. As soon as anyone suggests instructing an expert, you should alert the relevant budget holder immediately, and make sure you do not agree to anything without the decision maker's authority. The instructions to the expert must include details of the funding arrangements.

Court direction

If the court decides an expert is needed, it is very specific in its direction, naming the expert to be instructed, specifying the questions to be asked, and fixing dates for the letter of instruction to be sent for the report to be filed.

Letter of instruction

Drafting the letter of instruction is a lawyer's job, but if the local authority is involved in instructing the expert, you should have input and see the letter before it is sent. The Family Justice Council drafted sample questions to ask of experts of different disciplines and these

---

13   *JG v The Lord Chancellor & Others* [2014] EWCA Civ 656.

appear in Annex A[14] to the Practice Direction. These provide a good starting point, to be adapted to the case in question.

The expert receives a copy of all of the papers in the case. This must be kept up-to-date as new documents are filed.

Experts' duties

Experts have a duty to help the court, regardless of who instructs or pays them. They must:

- Provide advice conforming to the best practice of their profession (mavericks with unorthodox opinions are not appropriate in court).

- Answer the questions asked, taking all material facts into account.

- Provide an opinion independent of any of the parties.

- Confine themselves to matters within their expertise. If they are asked a question beyond their expertise, they should say so and advise whether another expert is required.

- Tell those instructing them of any change of opinion.

Experts' reports

The requirements for a report are set out in detail in Practice Direction 25B. Reports must include details of the author's qualifications and experience, include a confirmation that he has no conflict of interests and be verified by a statement of truth.

Opinions must be justified. The rules set out in detail what the expert must do including:

- taking into account relevant ethnic, cultural, religious and linguistic factors

- identifying the facts, literature and research relied on

---

14 Available at www.justice.gov.uk/courts/procedure-rules/family/practice_directions/practice-direction-25c-children-proceedings-the-use-of-single-joint-experts-and-the-process-leading-to-an-expert-being-instructed-or-expert-evidence-being-put-before-the-court#IDA54MGC, accessed 26 August 2014.

- describing his risk assessment and differential diagnosis processes, highlighting factual assumptions and deductions made

- highlighting any unusual, contradictory or inconsistent features of the case

- indicating whether any proposition in the report is a hypothesis (especially if controversial) or whether his approach is such as is generally accepted in his field of expertise

- giving reasons for any opinion expressed; a 'balance sheet' approach to the factors supporting or undermining an opinion can be very helpful.

Of course the report must be filed at court and served on the other parties, even if it directly contradicts the case of the party which commissioned it. Within ten days of receiving the report, if necessary, parties can send written questions to the expert to clarify the report. The answers are then treated as part of the report.

Experts' meetings

If there is more than one expert in a case, the court can direct them to meet to identify and discuss the expert issues, and, if possible, reach agreement or at least narrow the issues between them. They must then prepare a statement for the court setting out what they agree on, what they disagree on and why.

Attending court

Generally, the presumption is that the expert's report stands as evidence and courts will not direct experts to attend court to give oral evidence unless it is necessary in the interests of justice. Any party wishing the expert to come to court must apply before the IRH.

If several experts have to attend court, arrangements should be made so that all experts of the same discipline attend on the same day and they are usually allowed to sit in court to hear each other's evidence.

After you have received an expert's report and/or seen him in the witness box, make a note of your impressions of his strengths and weaknesses, and whether or not you would use him again. Either way, share the information with your colleagues – it could save a lot of time, money and anxiety in another similar case.

At the end of the case, the expert evidence is weighed in the balance by the court along with all of the other information in the case. The court in no way bound to follow the expert's view; as Ward LJ said,[15] 'the expert advises, but the judge decides'.

QUESTIONS FOR REFLECTION

- How can you be sure that experts are used only when necessary?

- How can your department ensure that information about court experts is shared and collated?

---

15   B *(Care: expert witnesses)* [1996] 1FLR 667 (Court of Appeal) p.670 D.

Chapter 9

Preparing for Court

Some – perhaps all – of this chapter may read like an egg-sucking manual for grandmothers. However, sometimes the obvious has to be stated, and every single one of these points has been missed by someone at some time.

Preparing your case

Paperwork

Re-read your statement(s). By the time of the final hearing, your initial statement could be six months old so you need to refresh your memory. Knowing exactly what you said and where you said it will help you enormously in the witness box. A consultant psychologist in the High Court was once referred to a particular paragraph in her own report and seemed almost surprised by what she had written. Clearly she had not re-read the document since she had written it several months earlier. Coupled with the fact that she repeatedly got the child's name wrong, her credibility was severely dented.

Re-read your file. When you live with a case for a long time, it is amazing how you can forget how things were. It can be like looking back over your life – you think you remember, but only when you look at old photos do the details come back. You need that fresh, detailed recall of the case, not a general hazy recollection.

Get your file in order. Make sure there are no loose pages and all papers are filed in the right place. Flag up significant documents or notes of important events, so you can turn them up quickly if need be. One expert witness went to the High Court carrying all her papers, not in a file but in a heap. Walking up to the witness box, she dropped the whole pile. The court had to rise while she and her instructing solicitor scrabbled about the floor picking up papers and trying to work out what order they should go in. You can imagine the judge's impression of that expert.

Take your file to the court building with you in case you need to check up on something which is not in your statement. Imagine being pressed about a precise detail which is not in your statement and that you cannot remember without checking the file – but the file is in the office, 40 miles away. How happy is the judge with you?

However, do not take your file into the witness box – you are unlikely to need it in any event as your statement is already in the court bundle – because anything you do take into the box can be inspected by the other parties. This could result in a fishing expedition, with everyone trying to trawl through your entire file to see if they can find anything of use to them, causing delay and irritation to all involved. If, however, during your evidence it becomes essential to check a particular point in your file, you can ask the judge for permission to find the relevant document, which you will then need to show to the other parties.

Focus your thinking

Among all the last-minute frantic preparations, take some time to reflect on exactly what the case is about. Get the key issues absolutely clear in your mind – what do you want to say to the court? Try summing up the essence of the case to a colleague in a few sentences. Think of three key things which, if nothing else, you want to get across to the court. Keep these in mind when you are in the witness box to keep you on track and help you deal with questions.

Get a clear mental image of the child concerned; remind yourself of what he looks like, his personality and his needs. Think of him before you go to court and keep him in mind throughout the case – after all, he is the reason you are doing this.

Meet your lawyer

Have a meeting with your legal team (known as a 'conference with counsel' if a barrister is instructed). Prepare together for negotiations outside court and for anticipated challenges in court. The lawyer is not allowed to coach you or rehearse your answers with you – you are the witness and it has to be your evidence, not the lawyer's – but there is nothing wrong with anticipating together how the case might proceed.

On the other hand, you can coach your lawyer. Help him to ask the right questions of you and the other witnesses, and suggest how he might deal with the parents, who you know far better than he does.

There are always some surprises in court and some questions you could never have anticipated. But some challenges are easily predicted: 'You only qualified a month ago, how can you be competent to handle this case?' 'The case was unallocated for three months so your authority could not have been very concerned – if the care was good enough then why not now?,' and so on. Some challenges are apparent from the evidence filed by other parties; for example, if the parents say that no one explained the concerns to them, or no services were provided.

Prepare for the challenges you expect, but don't practise your answers to such an extent that they sound like a rehearsed script. That comes across as false, and spontaneity is important in court. However, if you have not prepared for the challenges you know will come, you will have no spare brain space to deal with the genuine surprise developments.

Preparing yourself

Look the part

Knowing you look right gives you confidence. It is obviously sensible to decide in advance what you are going to wear and make sure everything is clean and in good order. If you expect to be in court for several days, you need some variation of outfits, all of which need to be clean and presentable. The last thing you need on the morning of court when you are already feeling anxious is to discover that your shoes need cleaning or you have just laddered your last pair of tights (take a spare pair with you, too). Some social workers complain that their salaries do not allow them to buy expensive suits, but designer labels are not required; it is quite possible to be smart on a budget.

It is amazing how, when you are already nervous, an apparently insignificant problem can throw you – one advocate, leaving for court very early one morning, got dressed in the dark to avoid disturbing her family. It was only when she arrived that, to her horror, she noticed that she was wearing one navy and one black shoe. For the rest of the day, she could not get out of her mind the idea that the entire court was focusing on her feet. Check your appearance before you leave home.

Think about the image you want to convey. Like it or not, first impressions are formed on the basis of appearance, and judges and magistrates are only human. The impression you want to convey is of a competent, serious professional and you may also want to counteract the stereotypical image of social workers, all baggy jumpers and sandals. These points might sound too obvious even to be made, but one Children's Guardian attended the High Court for a contested hearing wearing a denim dress and a bright red cardigan. Another Guardian appeared at court looking so unshaven, rumpled and grubby that at first sight the local authority's barrister mistook him for the abusive father in the case.

Colours should be sober, clothes formal (women need not wear skirts, smart trousers are perfectly acceptable) and appearance conventional; court is not the place for self-expression. After all, you are not there in your own right – you are representing your authority and your profession and you are there for the child. You want to be noticed and remembered for the quality of your evidence, not the way you look. A magistrate has recounted how a young female advocate appeared before the Bench in an extremely low-cut blouse. Imagine the first few minutes' discussion in the magistrates' retiring room – 'Did you see what she was wearing?' – not a word about the case!

Avoid potentially distracting items like dangly earrings or extravagant jewellery. Some judges and magistrates have 'pet hates' (such as pierced noses, eyebrows or tongues, joke socks or cartoon character ties) and antagonising the decision maker before you have even opened your mouth is not the best start. Having her hair dyed the colours of the rainbow for charity just before appearing in the High Court was not the best plan for one professional witness.

As well as image, think about comfort. It is a good idea to choose an outfit you know to be comfortable rather than wearing something for the first time. You may spend a considerable time in the witness box so five-inch stilettos may not be the best choice. Many people get hot when they are nervous, so consider wearing a sleeveless blouse or shirt under your jacket. One excellent and experienced witness's top tip for court work is 'wear comfortable pants'!

One advantage of wearing clothes of a type you might not normally choose is that it is like putting on a uniform or costume. It helps you get into role and to adopt your professional persona. It also means that when it is all over you can take it off again, get back to normal and relax.

Before leaving for court, look at yourself in a full-length mirror, stand up straight, look confident and see yourself as an assured, professional witness.

Eat, sleep and relax!

Think of the sort of advice mothers give before their offspring take exams and apply it to yourself. Getting a good night's sleep before court is a sensible start. The scent of lavender is reputed to aid sleep, as is using a hop pillow. Alternatively, a long soak in a hot bath, or having a milky drink before bed might work for you. Sitting up till 3 am 'revising' is never a good plan. Nutritionists all seem to be unanimous that a decent breakfast is essential.

If you are nervous, try using a relaxation tape, practise yoga or tai chi or do some exercise. Some swear by Bach Rescue Remedy. However, alcohol and drugs are best avoided. You know what works for you, and what temptations you are likely to succumb to, so be honest with yourself and be sensible.

Dealing with nerves

Nerves are natural, especially when performing a task for the first time – remember your first Case Conference or home visit – your first court appearance is no different. Judges and magistrates understand that witnesses are nervous, and remember that they too once had a first day in court. As for an interview or exam, a level of anxiety is natural, even desirable, and a witness who is not anxious to a degree is worryingly complacent and unlikely to perform well. Nerves can be healthy – they heighten your awareness and speed up your reactions. Many people think more clearly and quickly when they are keyed up. Adopt a positive attitude to your nervous feelings. Naturally, your stress will be more manageable if you are well prepared and know what to expect than if you are entering completely into the unknown.

Remember that no one else can see how you feel inside, and nerves often show far less than you imagine. It is amazing how often, after giving evidence in real life or role play, social workers say they felt terribly nervous, yet they appeared to observers to be quite calm and controlled.

Don't assume either that you are the only person in court who is apprehensive. Everyone there is performing an important task and should be conscious of that fact. Even the advocates are at least keyed up and some extremely agitated, though you might not know it. One highly experienced barrister when cross-examining constantly twiddles her fingers behind her back, betraying her stress. However, the judge sees only her utterly composed and confident front. The image to remember is that of the swan, gliding majestically on the surface, but paddling like fury underneath. You need to be that swan.

The judge or magistrates may well be anxious or worried too – imagine being in their shoes, having the responsibility of deciding a child's future. And never forget that the people feeling the worst of all in court are the parents, who stand to lose their child. Get your own stress into perspective.

Seek support

Rally your troops around you and ask for the support you need, both professional and personal. Make sure your colleagues and your family understand that you have a challenge ahead. Get whatever support and help you need from your supervisor. Have a reward or a treat ready for when it is all over – it gives you something to look forward to.

QUESTIONS FOR REFLECTION

- How do you cope with stress?
- How can you prepare yourself practically and emotionally for court?
- What support do you need?

Practical preparation

Clear your diary

A working day of 10 am to 4 pm doesn't sound too bad does it? You can surely fit in a meeting before court and a visit or two afterwards plus some quick phone calls at lunchtime, can't you? Oh no you can't!

Don't even try it – you will get distracted and delayed. You need to focus on the case in court and nothing else.

Court work is exhausting, so don't be surprised if you are much more tired than you expect; it is a very concentrated and intense day. Make sure your manager knows about your court commitment and makes necessary allowances, including ensuring that your other appointments are covered for you. It is impossible to concentrate on the court case if you are worrying about all your other commitments.

Prepare for a late finish

Court cases are usually scheduled to finish at 4 pm, but often more time is needed to allow a witness to finish his evidence or a suitable point to be reached for a break so the court sits on for a while. Courts have been known to continue sitting well into the evening, even late into the night on exceptional occasions.

Have contingency plans in place – you are hardly likely to give of your best if you are worrying about who will collect your child from school. One social worker involved in a case which was running over phoned school to explain she was stuck in court and her daughter should go to her auntie's after school. The next day the mortified teenager was approached by the pastoral care teacher asking if there were problems at home. Make it clear that you are in court as a witness or people assume the worst!

Plan your journey

Even experienced lawyers, amazingly, sometimes turn up at the wrong court – one barrister arrived at Colchester County Court only to find he should have been in Winchester. Nothing is less conducive to a calm professional performance than going to the wrong place, then arriving late, flushed and flustered and having to apologise before you start. Many towns have more than one court – Magistrates', Crown and County – all in different buildings, often on opposite sides of town. If you just rely on going to the town and asking directions to the court, you are bound to be sent to the wrong one. People are also unlikely to know where the Family Court is, as it is a relatively new invention.

Don't assume all hearings in the same case will be in the same court. The venue could change for any number of practical reasons, and sometimes this happens literally the day before the hearing.

Always check exactly where you should be going – get the court's address, phone number and a map – an old-fashioned paper map is a good back-up in case your satnav goes wrong on the day.

Few courts have parking facilities, so you need to know where to park. Have a couple of options available, remembering that things like market days or school holidays can have a considerable impact. Take into account traffic conditions at the time of day when you will be travelling, and listen to local radio or check the internet for news of any hold-ups. Don't forget loose change for meters. Similar considerations apply to public transport, including checking for cancellations and engineering works, as well as working out how to get from the station/bus stop to court.

Take your mobile phone with you, ensuring it is charged up and has enough credit. Programme in the telephone numbers for the court and your legal adviser so if you are running late you can phone ahead – at least then everyone is forewarned and you will feel less panicked. Remember, too, to know how to contact your senior wherever she will be on the day in case you need advice or a decision has to be made.

Double check the time of your hearing and don't assume that each hearing will be at the same time as the last. Professionalism includes being on time. There is work to be done outside court before the case starts and your advocate cannot do anything without you. Aim to arrive well before the case is due to start – half an hour is an absolute minimum unless your lawyer says otherwise. People will notice when you arrive. At least one usher keeps a mental note of when social workers arrive for court. When she hears the name of the worker on a case, she (invariably accurately) predicts whether he will arrive on time or keep everyone waiting. If the usher knows, you can be absolutely sure that everyone else in the court does too. What kind of reputation do you want to establish?

Contact your legal team the day before court to check on any last-minute changes or developments. Arrange where to meet your team. Some court buildings are enormous – the High Court in London is a Victorian Gothic rabbit warren – and it will not fill you with confidence if you start your day wandering like a lost lamb trying to find your team. Arrange a simple meeting point in advance, and know exactly who you are going to meet, including what they look like if you have not met before.

Find your way around the court building early in the day. Locate the toilets – it is amazing what nerves can do to the digestive system. Notice if there is more than one set of toilets available; sometimes it is worth walking a bit further to avoid an awkward encounter with a parent in the loo. Similar considerations arise for smokers. Find out where you are allowed to smoke. Be aware that you might end up sharing the smokers' corner with an angry parent or perhaps the parents' advocate; make sure you don't discuss the case and perhaps allow him to use the fellowship of the fag break to catch you off your guard. If you leave your team before the case is called in, remember to let them know where you are going – the case is bound to be called into court just when you have popped out for a cigarette.

At court

Behaviour outside court

Why does this matter? Think who might be watching. Courts rarely have enough individual conference rooms for all the parties in all the cases in court that day, and you may be in the same large waiting area as the parents and their advocates. Be aware of the impression you are conveying and put on your professional 'hat' right from the moment you enter the building. Remain conscious of your behaviour until you leave at the end of the day. You are representing your authority, the child, yourself and your profession all day, not just when you are in the witness box, and people who matter start forming impressions of you from the outset.

Picture one social worker sitting in the corner, reading and re-reading her files with an air of desperation, wringing her hands and biting her nails. How does the opposing advocate feel? The social worker has made his day already! Another worker arrives late looking a mess, keeps dropping things and has to borrow a pen. Does she look competent and organised? A third breezes in, chats loudly, has a laugh with the Children's Guardian, then shows everyone the latest photographs of her lovely children. How sensitive and professional does she appear?

Always be very mindful of confidentiality, especially if poor facilities mean that you are obliged to discuss matters in a general waiting area. Get out of earshot of others, but if this is impossible at least refrain from mentioning any names or identifying details.

Often you will see at court other professionals who are involved with you in a case other than the one which brings you to court – lawyers frequently find that they can catch up on several cases at once when they are at court, as all the local specialists are there. This can be useful, but make sure you never discuss a case in front of anyone not entitled to hear about it.

Seeing the parents at court

Social workers often ask whether they should talk to parents outside court. Clearly it would be inappropriate to have a jolly chat with the parents and then go into the witness box and outline their failings in glorious Technicolor. It may also create the wrong impression if you are seen to be talking earnestly to the parents, as if you are putting pressure on them to change their position. On the other hand, it would be frankly rude and unprofessional to ignore them completely, especially when you have been working closely with them for months.

The best course is to prepare in advance – tell the parents that when you are at court you will not be able to spend any time with them as you each have to talk to your lawyers and that the court day is different from your normal work with them. This way they will not be surprised when you greet them courteously, then move on. Except in cases where you judge that the parents may react in such a hostile manner that even greeting them would be provocative, you should at least acknowledge their presence.

Safety considerations

Aggression in court is in fact extremely rare – it is remarkable how the formal atmosphere of the court building can inhibit the behaviour of even the most difficult client. Parents are more often distressed and emotional than aggressive. However, it is always sensible to consider risks and if you have safety concerns, voice them as early as possible. Your health and safety are important considerations for your employer, quite apart from the fact that you are unlikely to perform well if you are worried.

Unfortunately, in one case the Court of Appeal[1] once showed a frankly scandalous lack of concern for social work witnesses,

---

1   *Re W (care proceedings) (witness anonymity)* [2003] 1FLR 329, Court of Appeal, p.334 [13].

expressing the view that the threat of violence from adults who faced permanent separation from their children was a 'professional hazard of social work and not exceptional'. If the case had concerned a police officer or nurse, would the court have described the threat of violence as just an acceptable risk of the job?

Despite this, the courts you appear in day to day are likely to have more concern for your safety. Family Courts do not, however, have security staff or police routinely available. Arrangements can be made if there is a significant risk, but the court must be notified in advance. Alert your legal representatives to your concerns immediately and ask them to put necessary measures in hand.

Always take sensible precautions for your own safety. Never be persuaded to give a parent a lift to court in your own car – even the most docile person may become agitated in such a stressful situation. Getting a client to court is the parent's solicitor's job; it is not your problem.

Waiting around before court can heighten tension. If there are enough interview rooms available, parents and the local authority can wait separately. If not, make sure that as much physical space separates the two sides as possible, and take particular care during breaks.

In court, the usual seating arrangements often mean that social workers and parents sit close to one another. These arrangements can be changed to ensure that there are other people, such as legal representatives, acting as a buffer zone between you. It is always possible to take sensible precautions; it just needs someone to think of it, so don't wait for someone else to raise the issue.

During the hearing, it is the court's job to ensure parties' behaviour is appropriate and not intimidating. Anyone who misbehaves could find himself excluded from court or held to be in contempt of court. In addition, the court will form a clear impression of the person concerned, and take it into account in its decision.

After court, make sure you are not followed to your car. If emotions are running high, either leave court quickly before the parents or wait until they are well clear of the building. Court buildings usually have more than one exit and it has been known on rare occasions for the local authority representatives to be ushered out of a staff exit to avoid confrontation.

Think carefully about your work with the family after court, particularly in the first few sessions after the court's decision when emotions may be raw.

Parents' lawyers

Never get into discussion with the lawyers for the other parties except in the presence of your own lawyer. It is, in fact, professionally improper for a lawyer to speak to another lawyer's client, so they should not attempt to approach you in any event. However, some seem to forget that social workers are effectively clients of the local authority's lawyers, so it is possible that someone may approach you quite genuinely – or they may be trying to take advantage.

Do not get drawn into discussions about the case and make it clear that you will only talk with your own representative present.

Waiting

One feature of court work is that there is always a lot of waiting around to be done. Courts have long lists of cases, many of which are listed at the same time and even if they are supposedly short matters, complications and emergencies often arise. Your own case may also need more time for discussions or for documents to be drafted before it is ready to go into court.

The key worker goes into court as soon as the case is called, but if you are a witness giving a discrete piece of evidence you have to wait outside court until it is your turn to go into the witness box. Your advocate will try his best to give you an idea of when you are expected to be heard, but estimating how long evidence will take is more art than science, and the witnesses before you may take more or less time than predicted.

Whenever you go to court, take something to keep yourself occupied while waiting. Re-reading your statement is a good start, but only goes so far – a bit like revising before an exam, there comes a point where no more will go in. Some have tried working on other cases which seems like a productive use of time, but the problem is that after a couple of hours' wait, you only have a moment's notice before you are in action, and your head is filled with the wrong case. Instead, it may be the perfect opportunity to catch up on your backlog of professional journals – that way, your mind stays on professional matters while not being distracted from the case in question.

Finally, the moment arrives when the usher announces your case. In care proceedings to preserve confidentiality the case number, rather than the parties' names, is called. After a long wait, it is all systems go in an instant.

Walking into court

The parties often take their places in court before the judge enters, and if so, you have time to find your place and settle down. You will probably sit beside or behind your advocate, depending on the layout of the court. It is a good idea to know in advance where you are supposed to sit, so ask your lawyer before you enter the court.

Witnesses other than the key worker have to remain outside court until their turn to give evidence. If you are in this position, the usher calls you by name into court. Everyone else, judge included, is already in place when you walk in, so all eyes are on you from the word go. The danger is that you walk into the courtroom looking like a rabbit blinking in the headlights unless you know in advance what the courtroom looks like and where you have to go.

If you have never been to the particular court before, arrive early and ask the usher (who usually wears a black gown) to show you the courtroom, explain who sits where and point out where the witness stand is. You can then start your 'performance' as a confident, composed professional from the moment you enter the courtroom.

Behaviour in court

Remember that the judge or magistrates can see the entire courtroom, not just the witness who is giving evidence at the time. They notice and take into account everything they observe – the parent who is angry or laughs inappropriately, the lawyer who has kicked off his shoes and is doodling, the social worker who huffs and puffs at other people's evidence. Your behaviour must be discreet, respectful and professional throughout.

Be an active client. Don't just sit back and let your lawyer get on with it. Discuss the progress of the case during any breaks and make suggestions including ideas of topics or questions to put to witnesses. If necessary, pass messages to him during the hearing, but do so discreetly – don't noisily tear out sheets of paper and wave them in front of him as this will distract and irritate the judge. It is your case, so make sure you play a full role.

Taking the witness stand

The next chapter considers the process of giving evidence.

QUESTION FOR REFLECTION:

- What practical steps can you take to prepare yourself for court?
- Can you devise a checklist to ensure you are ready?

Chapter 10

Giving Evidence

Presentation

The content of your evidence is obviously of vital importance. If you have a weak case, the best presentation in the world cannot save it. However, the converse is not true and poor preparation and presentation can undermine even a strong case.

When you take the stand to give your evidence, remember that a substantial percentage of your message is conveyed not through words but through voice and body language. It is not just what you say but how you say it that matters. Use every trip to court, whether as observer or participant, as a learning experience. Perform a critical observation of every witness you see – are they impressive or not? Why? What would you like to emulate or avoid? You might find the witness observation checklist in Appendix 5 helpful.

Impressive witnesses start as they mean to go on. From the moment they take the stand, they are composed, professional and assured.

Addressing your evidence

If you remember nothing else from this book, remember this. The single top tip to being an effective witness is to address everything you say to the decision maker(s). In family cases, this means the judge or magistrates; in the Crown Court, this means the jury.

Why?

- Think who needs to know the answer? Everyone else in the courtroom already knows what they think the outcome should be – and it matters not a jot. Only the judge's opinion matters, so speak to him, giving him the information he needs to make the right decision.

- How do the judge or magistrates feel if no one looks at them? Imagine being a magistrate, sitting in court while an advocate and witness have an apparently private exchange, looking at each other and never addressing you. How long would you remain engaged and concentrating on the case? Magistrates and judges are only human after all, and after a while are likely to feel excluded and struggle to maintain concentration.

- Cross-examination is all about control. The opposing advocate is trying to control you, and eye contact is perhaps the most powerful tool he has. If the witness is looking at him, the advocate can interrupt just by using body language. Try it yourself – you can stop someone in full flow just by taking in a breath, raising your eyebrows and signalling that it is your turn to speak. Most people are so polite that they obediently stop and allow you to take over. Advocates can also try to undermine the witness by feigning boredom, exasperation or incredulity at their answers – this does not work if the witness is not looking in their direction. Break the eye contact and you break the control.

- Who would you rather talk to – a hostile advocate or an at least neutral and possibly interested and encouraging judge or magistrate?

- You may get some feedback from the judge or magistrates – nods, frowns, puzzled looks – which may indicate how your evidence is being received and whether you are getting your message across, and you may even get an indication of approval or understanding. A foster carer was once cross-examined in an unnecessarily aggressive manner, and the magistrates physically leaned towards her – they would have given her a hug if they could! There was no doubt where the court's sympathy lay, and that the advocate was actually undermining his case by his aggression, but the witness would not have known that if she had only been looking at the advocate. Don't worry, however, if you get no feedback at all; it is a matter of personal style – some courts make a point of remaining studiously neutral, and at least one judge made everyone in court wonder if he was still alive, let alone listening (although of course he was).

- It shows courtesy to the court and gives everyone present the message that you are a professional witness who understands court etiquette.

Watch other people giving evidence, and you will see how effective this technique is and how witnesses who do not use it put themselves at a disadvantage. See if witnesses manage to maintain the technique throughout their evidence – sometimes people start well, but lose focus as they are challenged; or if they become anxious, riled or defensive; then the advocate gains the upper hand. As things become more challenging it becomes even more important to keep control.

Of course, it feels unnatural to be asked a question by one person and address the answer to someone else. We are trained from childhood to look at the person who is speaking to us, and witnesses sometimes worry that they seem rude if they do not look at the advocate. This is not the case, but in any event it is far better to risk rudeness to an advocate than to ignore the judge or magistrates. This technique does not come naturally, especially if you are feeling under pressure. So how is it done?

The key technique is to angle your body towards the judge/magistrates. Do this from the moment you enter the witness box, and make sure that every single word you utter, starting from the oath or affirmation, is addressed to them and no one else. Point your feet and hips towards the Bench and you will naturally look in that direction. When an advocate asks you a question, turn your head and shoulders towards him to receive the question, but as it is uncomfortable to stand in that twisted position for long, you naturally turn back towards the judge to give your answer. In many Family Courts, witnesses remain seated to give evidence so angle your chair, if you can, to face the Bench. If the seat is fixed, place your bottom so your body is angled towards the Bench.

As it is such an artificial exercise, it is not easy to use this technique without practice. Try it out in advance with two colleagues. Place yourself so that you cannot look at both colleagues at the same time. One person asks you questions, and you address the answers to the other, who listens passively without joining in the questioning. Start with unchallenging questions, such as your name, professional address and qualifications, just to get into the habit of looking from one to the other. Once you feel more comfortable about the principle, ask your questioner to step up a gear and start to tackle more challenging subjects, and to be provocative, perhaps raising religion, politics, the latest office reorganisation or something else likely to stir you up. Keep calm and continue to address your answers to the 'judge'.

Taking the oath/affirmation

The first thing you have to do as a witness is to take the oath (religious) or affirmation (non-religious). It does not matter which you choose, but know in advance which you want to do. Ushers often assume that witnesses will swear on the New Testament unless they say otherwise. Holy books and appropriate forms of words for other religions are available, but tell the usher in advance if this applies to you – otherwise you could be standing in the box in Court 1 waiting for the usher to run to Court 37 to get the relevant documents – hardly designed to calm your nerves.

At this point, the script is there for you and it is difficult to say the wrong thing, although it has been done – one social worker promised to tell a judge 'the truth, the whole truth and anything but the truth'. Use this chance to get yourself composed and get your voice working. Make sure you address the judge or magistrates from the word go, making eye contact although without fixing them with an unnerving, unblinking stare. Start as you mean to go on.

Should you sit or stand?

Witnesses always stand while taking the oath or affirmation, whichever court they are in. If you are in front of lay judges (magistrates) or a District Judge, the rest of the case is usually conducted with all participants (advocates and witnesses included) seated, whereas if you are before a Circuit or High Court Judge, witnesses are likely to remain standing to give evidence. However, there may be variations in local practice so check with your advocate before you go to court.

Sometimes a Circuit or High Court Judge may ask you if you would like to sit to give evidence. It is up to you, but bear the following points in mind:

- The advocates stand when asking you questions. It does not take much amateur psychology to work out who has the power if one person is sitting and the other standing. Do you want to put yourself at a disadvantage from the start?

- Traditional witness boxes are generally designed for a witness who is standing, not sitting. Unless they are particularly tall, witnesses practically disappear if they sit down in some courts. Try appearing authoritative when you are peering over the edge of the box!

- Anyone who sings will tell you that vocal production is generally better if you are standing upright so you can breathe freely and your diaphragm is not scrunched up as it may be when you are sitting down, especially if you hunch over.

- Standing up straight gives an air of confidence and helps remind you that you are performing an important task.

If there is a particular reason why it would be better for you either to sit or stand or to change position periodically during your evidence (for example if you have a bad back), don't just assume that you can do so; ask the court for permission.

Examination in chief

After the oath, the next stage is examination in chief, when you are asked questions by your own advocate. Your first task is to confirm your own name and professional address, so there is a good chance that you know the answer, however nervous you are.

Your advocate then asks you to confirm your statement(s). Do not take your own copy into the witness box but use the court bundle, which is indexed and paginated and contains copies of all the papers in the case. Sometimes there are problems with bundles such as incorrect pagination, missing pages or faulty photocopying. These are simple clerical errors, which easily occur – imagine photocopying and paginating thousands of pages – but they cause judicial irritation. None of this is your problem. Rise serenely above it. If you are asked to turn to a page in the bundle only to find that it is missing or looks wrong, don't soldier on, just point out the problem and let someone else sort it out.

Take your time to focus on the statement, make sure it is the right one, and remember that this is your opportunity to correct any mistakes.

Evidence in chief is brief, probably consisting of only a few questions to update the evidence since your last statement and to comment on any evidence filed after yours, such as the Guardian's report. Use this relatively straightforward stage to the full as an opportunity to ensure that you are facing the right direction and expressing yourself clearly.

The next stage is cross-examination, considered more fully in the next chapter.

Voice

We tend to take our voices for granted, and assume that speaking is something we learned to do when we were toddlers. In fact very few of us know how to breathe properly or ever give any thought as to how we actually produce the sound we make. We rarely hear ourselves as others hear us. Try recording yourself and play it back to hear how your voice sounds. How clearly do you speak? How quickly do you speak? Do you have any habits or 'you know', 'like', 'uh' vocal tics? Don't be the last person to know you have an irritating habit which you could easily overcome.

Our voices are vital tools of our trade which are too often neglected, so as part of your professional development programme consider going on a public speaking or presentation workshop or try singing or drama classes. How you speak in court is crucial for the most basic and obvious reason – the best evidence in the world is wasted if no one can hear it. Your voice is also an important part of the overall impression you convey. Imagine a witness who speaks in a timid, apologetic little voice which the court has to strain to hear. Does she inspire you with confidence in her professional expertise and competence? Or picture a witness who gabbles and races through his evidence – does he impress you as composed, organised and thoughtful?

Be aware of your surroundings and adjust your voice accordingly as courtrooms vary enormously in size. Some are no bigger than an average meeting room whereas others, especially in the higher courts, are large rooms with high ceilings. Do not rely on the microphones you see in some courts as they only record the evidence and do not amplify your voice.

You know whether you naturally have a quiet or strong voice. Bear in mind that sometimes an effect of nerves is that people speak more quietly than normal. If you cannot be heard in court, the judge or one of the advocates will ask you to speak up. This will not boost your confidence. If you have to be asked more than once it becomes irritating for all involved, judge included, and there comes a point where everyone gives up trying to persuade you to speak audibly and your evidence is effectively lost.

If you naturally speak quietly, it will feel strange to you to project your voice. You need to aim to speak at such a level that to you it feels too loud; to everyone else that will probably be about right. Practise as often as you can before going to court – with everything else to think about on the day, it is not the best moment to try speaking up for the first time. Start immediately, and try speaking out loudly in the privacy of your own home or car. Use the opportunity of any meetings you attend to make a conscious effort to project your voice more than usual. Find a large room and ask a helpful colleague to see how well you can be heard from a distance – not just once – such things take practice. Try saying the words of the oath or affirmation, giving your name, professional address and qualifications, then move on to a summary of your concerns about a particular child. The more you can get used to speaking out confidently, the better.

Get your voice working on the way to court. Sing in the shower, talk back to the radio in the car and practise any vocal exercises you know. As soon as you get in the witness box, start as you mean to go on and take the oath in a strong confident voice. Don't mumble – open your mouth and enunciate clearly.

Remember that you will be giving evidence for some time and you need to sustain your volume throughout. Sometimes witnesses start confidently enough then lose momentum and volume as they go along. It can be a real indicator that a witness is tiring or losing confidence if her voice starts to drop, and that only encourages a cross-examining advocate, so throughout your evidence periodically remind yourself to keep speaking up. If you feel your confidence starting to sap, that is the time to redouble your efforts to at least sound confident.

Diction

This is not an elocution exam. You do not have to speak the Queen's English or have impeccable diction, but you do have to be understood.

Accents often become stronger through nerves, and this is exacerbated if you also speak quickly or mumble. If you are aware that you have a marked accent, don't feel you have to put on a voice which is not your own, but be very careful to enunciate as clearly as you can and to speak at a measured pace. Again, a frank colleague can help you practise.

Pace

Another common nervous reaction is to speak too quickly. Witnesses sometimes gabble in the anxiety to get out everything they want to say, but end up defeating the object as their evidence gets lost in the rush. Before lay judges, usually the only record of the proceedings is the handwritten note kept by the clerk. Clerks have been heard to cry out 'watch the pen!', meaning do not start on the next sentence until he has caught up. Even in courts where proceedings are tape recorded, everyone (judge included) keeps their own notes of evidence. While you should not go at dictating speed, people still need to be able to keep up with you.

If you know you speak quickly at the best of times, make a particular effort to slow down and to pause more often. It may have to feel unnaturally slow to you to get to the point where it sounds right to others. Try recording yourself and taking notes when you play it back – can you keep up?

Start by reading the oath at a measured pace and be sure to keep it up. As with volume, witnesses often start well, then forget as time goes on, especially if they become in any way animated. Witnesses losing their cool – whether riled, defensive or emotional – tend to speed up, so this is a real signal to cross-examining advocates that the witness is losing composure and it is time to turn up the heat.

Silence is also part of communication. Don't be afraid to pause. Take your time to think; avoid rushing. Take a deep breath as this not only helps you to speak more strongly but also calms your nerves. Try to breathe from your diaphragm rather than taking shallow, panting breaths. If your mouth gets dry, take a sip of water (there should be a glass on the witness stand – if there isn't, ask for one). You can also make your mouth water by running your tongue over the front of your teeth, gently biting the tip of your tongue or just by imagining yourself sucking on a lemon.

QUESTION FOR REFLECTION

- Could you benefit from any training to improve your vocal skills?

Tone

As for written work, the message is conveyed not just by what you say, but how you say it. Listeners pick up a lot of subtle information about you and how you are feeling from your voice. Keep calm and controlled – avoid being pompous, defensive, angry or emotional. Remember, too, to keep the audience interested by varying your pitch and tone – no one wants to listen to a monotonous robot for long (just think of an interview with many sports stars). It helps if you remember that you are talking to real people who just happen to be magistrates, telling them what you know, rather than giving a speech to a vast impersonal audience. Keeping your child client in the forefront of your mind will help you to maintain the interest and conviction in your voice.

Language

The language you use in the witness box is important, first to ensure that your evidence is readily understood by everyone in court and second to convey an air of professionalism and competence.

Avoid jargon. Specialist terms may not be understood by everyone in court or, worse still, people listening may think they know what a term means, but may have misunderstood it completely. A magistrate who does not understand a term is unlikely to want to look foolish by asking what it means. Stick to plain, ordinary English to get your message across.

However, do retain a level of formality in your speech. You are giving evidence on oath, not chatting to your friends; this is a formal, important occasion. Avoid vulgarity. You might think this so obvious that it does not need to be said, but apparently not. One consultant psychiatrist giving evidence in care proceedings said, 'If you treat children like shit, they turn into shit.' What would be your reaction on hearing that from an expert witness? Probably not very different from the judge, who exclaimed, 'That is language I might expect to hear from a juvenile delinquent, not a consultant psychiatrist!' and demanded an apology. You can imagine how much reliance the judge placed on that witness's evidence.

It can sometimes be necessary to use a swear word if repeating the precise words someone used. It can be significant evidence, for example, that the child's speech is very limited save for a fluent knowledge of vulgarities. Or it can be an indicator of a parent's ability to co-operate with professionals if you are subjected to a string of obscenities on every visit. It is no good being coy, saying that someone 'was rude' or 'used abusive language' – that is far too subjective. Instead, signal to the court that this is not the language you would normally use in court – you could say, 'If I may, I will use her exact words...', then go ahead and tell the court what was said. Everyone in court is an adult and it is unlikely to be the first time they have ever heard bad language.

Posture and body language

Stand or sit up straight. If you are standing, adopt an open stance with your feet slightly apart, in line with your hips – this should feel comfortable and make you feel grounded. Keep your shoulders back and avoid hunching over. Keep your chin up (literally and metaphorically) and look people confidently in the eye. Before you go to court, visualise yourself looking assured and composed and retain that mental image. If you are sitting, sit up straight, neither hunched over nor slouching – take care not to become too relaxed.

Be careful what messages you convey with your hands – they can aid communication or add expression with an occasional gesture to reinforce a point, but they can also give away nerves or agitation if you tap your fingers, wring your hands or grip desperately to the edge of the witness box. You would look disrespectfully casual if your hands were in your pocket, or defensive if you stood with your arms folded. Your hands can distract attention if they wave around as if you are doing semaphore, or if you constantly repeat a particular gesture like a visual tic. Some witnesses gesture more when they get carried away or lose their composure – another give-away sign for the predatory advocate. Some of us have a habit of fiddling with our pens. It is very difficult to retain professional composure while desperately trying to rub ink off your fingers and to address the court with an air of authority despite having bright blue hands (a painful personal experience). If you are an inveterate pen fiddler, take a pencil – at least they don't leak.

Don't think that you have to stand in the witness box immobile like a soldier standing to attention, but do be aware of what your posture and gestures communicate. Some people find it comforting to rest their fingertips lightly together (not clamped together as if you are praying for help); it is suggested that this makes the 'chi' energy flow smoothly through the body.

Become aware of your own habits – stand in front of a full-length mirror and describe to yourself in the mirror your concerns for a particular child. Watch yourself while you are speaking and note your own body language. Ask a helpful colleague to watch you and be honest about how you come across or, better still, if you can bear it, video yourself.

QUESTION FOR REFLECTION

- How can you become aware of and improve your non-verbal communication skills?

Answering questions

Think again about how you want to appear as a witness. Words like calm, professional, reasonable, clear and thoughtful probably spring to mind.

Listen to the question

Focus carefully on the question you are actually asked. Sometimes witnesses seem to hear the start of the question, then jump to their own conclusion of what the advocate is asking. Concentrate on the exact words the advocate uses and listen out for subtle differences – for example, you might be happy to agree that a parent *listens* to your advice, but not that she *takes* your advice.

Ask for clarification or repetition where necessary. If you do not hear the question, ask for it to be repeated. If you do not understand the question, don't guess at what you think it meant – you might have the wrong end of the stick. It is not your problem if the advocate cannot express himself clearly, and it is not your job to help him out. Ask for the question to be repeated or rephrased. You will probably find that no one else in court understood it either! Advocates hate being asked to repeat a question, especially when they know that it wasn't the most elegant question ever posed.

Take your time

You are not on Mastermind – it is not an exercise to answer as many questions as possible in a limited time. You will not get it over with more quickly by rushing; on the contrary, ill-considered answers could lead to you spending longer in the witness box. Consider each question and your response to it. You do not have to answer instantly, and should not be afraid of a moment or two of silence in the courtroom. If you feel uncomfortable pausing when all eyes are on you, try taking a sip of water (just a sip, not huge gulps or you will need a comfort break), or looking for a moment at your statement in front of you. You could try using a phrase along the lines of 'let me take a moment to consider', so that the room is not in silence, but you are still giving yourself time to think.

If you don't know the answer – say so. Never make things up. Don't speculate or hypothesise. Don't ask, as one witness did, 'Can you give me a clue?' If you cannot remember, say so, but do feel free to use your statement to refresh your memory – court is not a memory test.

Answer the question

Do answer the question actually asked. Don't try to avoid it, give a stock answer no matter what the question may be, or answer the question you wish you had been asked. Think of politicians you have seen doing this in interviews and remember how irritating it is. No one is fooled.

Don't try to second-guess where the advocate is going. He has a game plan and has thought questions out several moves ahead, like a game of chess, but you don't have to. Trying too hard to spot the direction of the advocate's questions and his ultimate objective can result in a witness looking suspicious or defensive. Take each question as it comes and consider your answer carefully before giving it.

Your job is to answer questions, not to ask them – don't answer a question with a question and never get into an argument.

Know your boundaries

Know the limits of your expertise and of your role in the case. Do not answer a question which is not properly one for you – resist the temptation to try to help out. If a question should be properly addressed to another witness, say so. For example, as a social worker, do not attempt to answer a medical question, but suggest that the advocate should ask the paediatrician. The advocate could be deliberately inciting you to stray beyond your expertise, only then to criticise you for doing so. If your only role was to observe contact, don't get drawn in to making comments about the child's care plan – the advocate may be trying to divide and rule, playing one witness off against another.

Focus on the child

Always remember what – and who – the case is about. The issue is how the child has been treated and her welfare. It is not a trial of your competence as a worker or the efficiency or otherwise of your authority's services. Nor is it a trial of the behaviour or personalities of the parents – these are only relevant in so far as they affect the child. It is not a question of whether the parents are morally guilty – they may be utterly blameless, but still unable to care for their child. Try not to get distracted onto other topics – this might be the advocate's very objective – and always try to bring your thoughts and evidence back to what is relevant for the child.

Don't be monosyllabic

Occasional one-word answers can be refreshing, but if your evidence simply consists of single-word responses you fail in your main task of informing the court and could give the impression that you have something to hide or simply do not trust yourself to answer more fully.

Don't ramble

Answers which are too long can lose the court's attention and often stray away from the point and lose coherence. Witnesses who waffle seem unfocused and disorganised, giving the impression that they are not clear thinking in their work either. Keep your answers to the point.

Above all, keep your cool

Stay calm and professional throughout. Keep in control of your emotions. Never show yourself to be angry, upset or irritated, even if that is how you feel inside. Take a deep breath, count to ten, take a sip of water, and always remember to look at the judge or magistrates. Remember you are not on trial; you are there to do a job for the child.

QUESTIONS FOR REFLECTION

- What are your strong points as a witness?

- What do you need to work on? How can you practise? What training should you request?

Chapter 11

Cross-examination

What is cross-examination for?

Contrary to popular belief, cross-examination is not designed just to satisfy lawyers' sadistic tendencies. Courts are charged with making very difficult and significant decisions. Evidence needs to be tested to ensure that it is reliable. Where more than one version of events is put forward, the court's need to ensure that each is rigorously probed is even more acute.

Asking questions is a natural way to check whether what is being said is true or not – you have certainly done this yourself. Imagine you are faced with a broken window, a football and two children each denying responsibility – what do you do? No doubt you ask each child questions, including a few trick questions, and from their responses (what they say and how they say it) you judge what really happened. The simple idea that the answers to questions illuminate the path to the truth lies at the heart of our trial system.

In court, however, the questions are asked not by the neutral arbitrator, but by someone who is partisan. His aim is not to get to the objective truth but to his client's subjective version of it, while at the same time undermining the accounts put forward by the other parties. This is achieved by cross-examination, which is a vital part of the right to a fair trial. Imagine for a moment being the parent in care proceedings, risking the loss of your child. Wouldn't you want your advocate to ask every possible question and use any available tactic? Do not, therefore, be surprised if that is what parents' advocates do. It is a legitimate part of the process, and it is right as a matter of principle that your case should be strenuously tested. Remind yourself of this if you ever feel upset or angered by a question – wouldn't you do the same thing if the positions were reversed? The advocate is just doing his job, and you must do yours.

In care proceedings where there are multiple parties, every witness is cross-examined by a number of advocates, each approaching the case from a different angle. Imagine you are seeking a care order with a care plan of adoption. You are cross-examined by advocates on behalf of:

- the mother, who argues that your concerns are exaggerated and the child should return to her

- the father, who acknowledges some concerns, but blames the mother and says the child should live with him instead

- the grandmother, who agrees neither parent can cope, but argues the child should come to her instead of being adopted

- the child on the instructions of the Guardian, who accepts your concerns and supports a care order but argues for fostering with contact, not adoption.

The different objectives and standpoints of each party determine the questions each advocate asks you.

Cross-examination questions

As they are designed to achieve a particular outcome, cross-examination questions are different from questions in normal life. Generally we ask a question because we do not know the answer and genuinely want to find out, but when a lawyer asks a question in cross-examination, he already knows what the answer will be, or at least what he wants it to be. No advocate should venture into the unknown (known as 'going on a fishing expedition') because he could get an answer which damages his case.

An advocate wants to control the witness – he knows what he wants her to say and his objective is to make her say it. It is no surprise, therefore, to find that cross-examination is full of closed and leading questions. The advocate avoids open questions which put the witness in control and give her the chance to repeat her evidence in chief, emphasising yet again all of his client's faults and failings.

Advocates also know that information is not just conveyed by the words spoken, but also by the witness's demeanour. Questions may be designed, therefore, not just to make the witness say a certain thing, but to behave in a certain way, for example to show herself to be judgmental or arrogant.

You are not a marionette. The advocate wants to control you, but you do not have to let him. His role is to try to shape the evidence his way; your role is to give information – the truth, the whole truth and nothing but the truth – to the court. You do have to answer the advocate's questions, but you do not have to dance to his tune – make sure the evidence you give is your own and as you want it to be.

How advocates prepare

Imagine yourself as advocate for the parent in a case you know well. What is your objective? How do you approach the task?

For a start, an advocate must have a detailed knowledge of the case. She reads and re-reads every page of the bundle and knows exactly what each witness has written in evidence, and how it all fits together – she especially knows where there are gaps, weaknesses and contradictions. If you are the key worker, you have the same bundle as she does, so you should be just as well informed and well prepared. Remember, though, that you have an advantage over even the best advocate – you were there, you saw things with your own eyes, you know this child and this family – she only knows the papers. You should know your own case more intimately than any advocate ever can.

Based on her client's instructions, the advocate develops her own case theory – the version she wants the court to accept – and designs both broad strategy and detailed tactics to get her there. She seeks to undermine the case overall and to challenge the witnesses' credibility and the details of their evidence. She also makes the most of any evidence favourable to her client, no matter who it comes from. She knows what she wants to achieve with each witness individually and how that fits into the whole picture she is trying to create for the court; sometimes she may seek to play one witness off against another. She plans her cross-examination of each witness, aiming to start and finish on a high note every time.

Emphasising strengths

You can always expect this. If there have been 20 difficult, distressing contact sessions and just one which was acceptable, it is no surprise if the parents' advocate emphasises every single detail of the acceptable one. This should already be fully acknowledged in your statement so you can simply refer to the concessions you have already made. Don't be grudging about positives – sometimes social workers seem to fear that anything complimentary said about a parent will undermine their case. In fact the reverse is true – the court appreciates a fair social worker who generously acknowledges a parent's strengths. On the other hand, you must not allow the advocate to blow these positives out of all proportion; you need to keep a sense of balance.

If, however, your statement does not mention positives which should fairly be there, you will be portrayed as selective and unfair. In a case involving a young and vulnerable mother, the worker filed a statement full of criticisms and negatives with no concessions. In cross-examination, the worker was asked to outline some of the mother's strengths, which she did, fairly and generously. She was then asked where those points were in her statement. An uncomfortable look crossed her face as she realised that her statement said nothing positive about the mother. She had to concede that this information was not there and it should have been. The questions then followed: if you have left out such important information, what else have you conveniently forgotten? Is your evidence the whole truth or just the bits of the truth you want the court to hear? And if you are so critical and negative towards this vulnerable young mum, is it any surprise that she found it difficult to work with you? Shouldn't there now be an adjournment with a change of worker to give this mum a fair chance to keep her baby?

Undermining the local authority's case

Contradicting factual evidence

The factual evidence is the foundation of the case. Opinions and recommendations are based on the facts. Therefore, if the court can be persuaded that the factual matrix you rely upon is inaccurate, your conclusions naturally fall. Imagine, for example, a case where a baby has suffered a subdural haematoma. Your case is based on medical opinion that this is a shaking injury. If the parents persuade the court that in fact what happened was they accidentally dropped the child down the stairs, the whole case folds. The advocate's objective is to persuade the court to accept his clients' version of the facts.

Sometimes advocates challenge the truth of the local authority's evidence by putting forward a different version of events ('You say the child is indifferent to mother at contact, but in fact she runs to her with open arms'). They rarely suggest that professional witnesses are actually lying – that would alienate the court and generally is implausible – why would a professional lie? More often, they suggest that you 'might be mistaken', or that 'on reflection, perhaps things might have been different', or you might have 'misunderstood or misinterpreted' things.

Advocates might offer you an alternative scenario and invite you to accept it, sometimes expressed as 'I put it to you that…'. Does the advocate really expect you to change your mind? Does he seriously think you will say, 'Well, now I think about it, you're right' or, 'You guessed it, I made it all up'? He would probably fall over if you did, so why does he ask the question? In fact, he is professionally obliged to put his client's case to you. Where the court is faced with two or more competing versions of events, the witnesses must each be given the chance to comment on the other's account. He cannot later call his client to give her evidence that you were the one who slapped the child not her, without first giving you the opportunity to consider and confirm or deny that evidence. Do not be concerned, therefore, about 'I put it to you…' questions. Do not get offended that you are being called a liar. All you need to do is to consider the question and calmly reply that you do not agree with the advocate's proposition and confirm that things were as described in your statement.

However, do not adopt a reflex response of always disagreeing with the advocate. Take time to consider the question as there may be exceptional circumstances where you might want to accept his suggestion. One health visitor's report included a list of the child's height and weight measurements. There was evidently a mistake in one entry as the figures indicated the child had lost height one month, a unique medical phenomenon. Somehow this had slipped everyone's notice until cross-examination. The advocate invited the witness to accept that this figure must be a typing error, but she insisted it accorded with her records; so it was suggested that her reading on that date had been inaccurate or her equipment was faulty. Instead of gracefully accepting that there must be some mistake, she refused to concede any errors whatsoever and kept on insisting that her evidence was accurate, in spite of the obvious offence to common sense. By so doing, she undermined her own credibility.

Sometimes, the advocate might challenge a witness's recall by asking in considerable detail about a particular incident seeking to establish that she cannot recollect all or part of the event, and thereby suggesting that her recall is suspect overall. Even if your recall is accurate, the advocate may try to show that it is selective – that you have only remembered or noted those elements which suit your case, showing you to be both judgmental and an unreliable historian. If you rely on notes, particularly if the event was some time ago, the accuracy of those notes could be challenged, especially if they were not contemporaneous (that is, made at the time) but are a neatened up and edited version prepared for the file. However, the advantage you have over the parents is that you do at least have notes which were, one hopes, made close to the event. If your recall can be challenged when you do have a record, imagine how much more forcefully the same challenge applies to the parents. Parents' solicitors often advise them to keep their own records and diaries of events during the course of proceedings, just as professionals do, but sadly they rarely manage to put that advice into practice.

Contradicting the interpretation of the facts – challenging opinions

If the facts themselves cannot successfully be challenged, the next possibility is to tackle how those facts are applied. The advocate might challenge the witness's expertise and entitlement to express opinions at all. He will do this, if at all, at the outset of the witness's evidence and the court will hear details of the witness's qualifications and experience to determine whether she is an expert. If not, her opinions will be excluded.

Another tactic is to try to undermine the witness's level of expertise – accepting that she has some, but not such as to entitle her to give an authoritative view. This is an obvious approach where, for example, a newly qualified social worker has a different opinion from an experienced Guardian. By emphasising the social worker's lack of experience, the advocate could undermine her confidence as well as suggesting to the court that her recommendations should be treated with caution.

An expert in one field is not entitled to express opinions in another. An advocate may try to entice you to do so, relying on your natural inclination to be helpful – do not be tempted; know your own limits. If a social worker expresses the view that the mother was suffering from paranoid delusions (without a psychiatric diagnosis in place), the next question will be as to when the worker qualified as a psychiatrist as she omitted to mention this in her statement. If a witness does not know her boundaries, her credibility can be undermined.

Even if the witness's expertise is accepted, her opinion can be challenged by suggesting that the facts do not lead logically to the conclusion drawn, that certain factors have been given too much or too little weight, or that an alternative conclusion is equally, or more, valid.

Research or theories quoted can be challenged by arguing that the material chosen is inappropriate for the case, and putting forward alternatives; by arguing that the right theory has been wrongly applied; or simply by testing the social worker's depth of knowledge of the tools she has used – if a shaky foundation is exposed, the whole basis of the reasoning starts to crumble.

How an advocate approaches a case

Baby Jack's case turns on physical and emotional neglect. The evidence includes information on unhygienic home conditions and on the failure of his mother, Kate, to provide him with adequate physical or emotional care or stimulation. Unsuccessful efforts to improve Kate's parenting skills are detailed.

Kate denies many of the allegations but accepts that, due to postnatal depression, she has sometimes been less responsive than she should have been. She has not found social workers helpful – on the contrary she feels criticised, undermined and disempowered. Now she is receiving treatment for depression and feels able to cope.

What does Kate's advocate want to achieve and how might she do it?

Overall objective
Resist the making of a care order – aim to end proceedings with no order being made.

Case plan:

Step 1 – positives:

1. Emphasise Kate's strengths.

2. Show Kate is reasonable and acknowledges some problems.

3. Her postnatal depression (the cause of the problems) is now being treated.

Step 2 – undermine Social Services' case:

1. Establish problems were exaggerated.

2. Show that the social worker's approach was unhelpful.

Strategy

1. With each witness get credit for Kate's positive qualities and good aspects of parenting (if witnesses are balanced and fair, these points should be conceded; if not, this helps towards points 4 and 5). Supplement this with Kate's own sympathetic demeanour in the witness box.

2. Get acknowledgement that Kate recognises the problems, showing insight.

3. Stress the medical explanation for difficulties.

4. Put each incident/criticism Kate denies to social work witnesses with the alternative version of events and invite concessions; isolate and minimise each individual concern; suggest that the social worker is exaggerating concerns, imposing unrealistic standards and being judgmental.

5. Dissect and criticise the social worker's approach – find fault with services offered and the failure to provide different services (for example, the failure to spot depression); attack the manner of delivery (critical and judgmental, not supportive and constructive). Use the social worker's demeanour in the witness box to reinforce this.

Style of questioning

Advocates adopt a variety of styles. To some extent this is a reflection of their personalities and approach. However, better advocates have at their disposal a range of styles and techniques and choose the most effective for the particular witness or the particular moment. It can be disconcerting for a witness who thinks she has got used to the advocate's gentle questioning style suddenly to be faced with a waspish strike, or for a witness who has been warned that a particular advocate is usually aggressive to find a smiling, coaxing questioner.

Aggressive and bullying questioning

Most inexperienced witnesses expect cross-examination to be aggressive; they imagine they will be torn to shreds and left weeping. In fact this is extremely rare. Aggressive or histrionic advocacy is generally counter-productive in the Family Court – there is no jury to impress, and judges favour a less adversarial approach. If they feel a witness is being unfairly intimidated or bullied, they will step in to stop it, and their sympathies then lie more with the witness than the advocate.

On the whole, therefore, family advocates tend not to be aggressive or bombastic, instead trying to be (or at least to appear) reasonable and likeable. Sometimes, however, an advocate might choose to be aggressive, challenging or provocative. This might be because:

- He wants to provoke a particular response from the witness. Imagine the local authority's barrister cross-examining an allegedly aggressive and abusive father. The statements include pages of description of the man's intemperate and unpleasant behaviour, but what could be more powerful than letting the magistrates see him in action for themselves? The barrister might deliberately aim to wind him up and let him go. This should not apply directly to a professional witness, and no amount of provocation should induce an angry or aggressive response from a social worker. However, it might be part of a parent's case that the social worker is hostile, defensive and unwilling to listen, or judgmental and biased. These attitudes might be shown up by aggressive questioning – not just through what the witness says, but the manner in which she says it.

- His client has specifically instructed him to be challenging. The lawyer might have advised his client that there is no realistic chance of success, but the client wants to fight nonetheless and wants the social workers to have a hard time in the process. The advocate is doing little more than going through the motions, making a show for his client to give him his day in court.

- The advocate is inexperienced and nervous or is used to appearing in the Crown Court where grandstanding is more acceptable, and he is simply not attuned to the atmosphere of the Family Court.

- He really has no good points to make and tries to make his case look impressive by lots of sound and fury, signifying nothing.

How to deal with an aggressive advocate

Never forget that addressing your answers to the judge breaks eye contact with the advocate and thus his control. You will feel calmer talking to the judge rather than to the unpleasant advocate.

Whatever you do, never ever rise to the bait – that is exactly what the advocate wants you to do, so do not give him the satisfaction. Do not get involved in an argument, answer a question with a question or get defensive. Stay calm at all times and retain your composure.

Take your time. Aggression often requires a fast pace to be sustained, so break the rhythm. Pause, consider the question, take a deep breath, look at the papers or take a sip of water.

Feel sorry for the advocate – if aggression is his best tactic, he must have a very weak case. He is only trying to do his job. Remember that the court is likely to be unimpressed by him and their sympathies will be with you. Don't risk antagonising the court yourself by your demeanour.

Always remember that the case is not about you – it is about the child. Keep your mind on your objective.

Gentle and smiling questioning

This can be one of the most effective approaches, well-suited to the Family Court. A witness who expects a tough challenge can be lulled into a false sense of security by an apparently unchallenging and sympathetic advocate. This is a particular danger in those courts where everyone is seated. One experienced social worker was taken completely off her guard by a kind, friendly advocate. The layout of the particular courtroom was such that advocate and witness were sitting opposite each other. The witness forgot to address the Bench, and looked at the friendly, open face of the advocate. It was like an informal chat and the witness was clearly dangerously relaxed; she had forgotten that she was giving evidence on oath to the court. She was then completely wrong-footed when the trap into which she had been so smilingly led was sprung.

Likewise, a mother who allegedly had no control over her very young but dangerously wayward children proved the local authority's case for them thanks to gentle questioning. Criticising or challenging her would have provoked a defensive response, so the local authority's advocate sympathised with how difficult it must be to look after these children and what a hard time she must have had. The mother told him about all her troubles, including recounting events unknown up to that point even to the social workers, encouraged all along by the advocate's gentle prompting. She had no idea of the damage she had done to her own case.

How to deal with gentle, friendly cross-examination

Do not be fooled or lulled into thinking that this is anything other than a rigorous test of your evidence. Remain on your guard – without overdoing it and becoming defensive or looking suspicious. Give each question the same degree of consideration and respect as you would if it were asked in a more overtly challenging manner.

It can be very tempting to try to help out someone who seems to be pleasant and friendly – resist the temptation. Don't be drawn into answering questions beyond your expertise or knowledge, into speculation or hypothesis ('if my client manages to stay off drugs') or into comparing one client with another ('many of your other clients must be much more difficult than my client').

It is always nice to be able to agree with someone, and the friendly advocate often puts propositions to the witness which she can agree to – he takes her by the hand and leads her down the garden path. Before you take each step, make sure that you really do want to go in that direction. Often, the first few steps are small and simple and it is no problem to go along with the advocate – but don't get into the habit of agreeing, and watch out for the subtle detour in the path or the giant step too far at the end. Never agree to statements which you would not make of your own accord.

Even if you do agree, avoid getting into the habit of replying 'yes' to each question as this leads to the temptation to say 'yes' when the answer should be 'no'. Try using different words for each answer – 'correct', 'that's right', 'quite so', 'I agree'.

Never let yourself be flattered. If an advocate who is not your own starts emphasising how skilful you are or how brilliantly you have worked, remember that he is doing this for a reason, which may not be clear even at the end of your evidence, because he may be building up ammunition to fire later at someone else. For example, sometimes parents have a better relationship with one professional, perhaps a social work assistant, than another, such as the key worker. The advocate's case might be that the difference in relationships is due to a difference in competence between the two workers. If only all the professionals were as competent and helpful as the social work assistant, his client could keep her child. He might therefore be full of compliments to the assistant who, not seeing the rest of the case, is pleased she had an easy ride – she does not see the sting in the tail, reserved for the key worker.

Other techniques

There are many other ways of irritating or disconcerting a witness – a patronising or superior attitude can be provocative. The advocate might change styles from one question to the next, to put the witness off her stride. He might change pace, or ask quick-fire questions one after another to give the witness little time to think. Questions and answers take on a rhythm and those watching end up doing the Wimbledon head movement. Don't allow your pace to be dictated by the advocate. Just because he is going quickly does not mean you have to – you do not have to dance to his tune.

At other times, the advocate might introduce long pauses between questions or remain silent when you have finished your answer, implying your answer is incomplete or making you feel uncomfortable with the silence and obliged to fill it up. Don't give in to this temptation. If you have finished your answer, don't say anything else – the ball is in the advocate's court, and the judge will become impatient if he takes too long before his next question.

Sometimes an advocate might give an exaggerated or dramatic reaction, raise his eyebrows, or make a great play of noting down your answer in his book, repeating your words in a questioning or sarcastic tone or saying things like 'really?' or 'I see' in an apparently significant manner. Alternatively, he may pretend not to understand your answers. This may mean nothing at all. It may be designed to unsettle you and make you wonder whether you have just made a faux pas – it could even be that he is simply playing for time while thinking of his next question, so do not let it unnerve you.

Advocates are taught not to convey any signal except on purpose. If an advocate reacts to a response from a witness, it is done deliberately to make a point to the court or as part of his strategy for handling the witness (unless he is not very good at his job and cannot contain his own reactions). If something goes wrong in a case and the answer which emerges has disastrous implications for his case, the advocate is supposed to 'ride the bumps' and continue to appear utterly calm and collected as if nothing had happened. This is hopelessly undermined if, behind him, his client is holding her head in her hands, grimacing, gesticulating or otherwise giving the game away. Remember this in court – don't undermine your own advocate's efforts if things don't go smoothly in your case; keep a poker face at all times. The judge does not just look at the witness box – he sees everyone in court and takes it all in.

Advocates will use to their advantage any errors you may have made, however minor. This is another reason to double check your statement, as having the opposing advocate drawing attention even to a small mistake such as an incorrect date or error in numbering can make you feel a fool and undermine your confidence.

However, don't be afraid of lawyers. Not all advocates are good at their jobs – like any other profession, some are brilliant, some awful and most are pretty workmanlike. Even a superb advocate can have a bad day or ask a stupid question – lawyers sometimes get things wrong like everyone else. Don't be perturbed if it seems the opposing advocate isn't very good – you might just be right!

Re-examination

If you feel that all has not gone well for you in cross-examination, remember that your advocate has the chance to re-examine you. This is an opportunity to clarify or correct any points raised in cross-examination or to limit any damage done. If the Children's Guardian is supporting your case, her representative's cross-examination can perform the same function.

Remember, in any event, that the whole case does not stand or fall on your performance in the witness box – all the other written and oral evidence is taken into account as well.

After all the local authority witnesses have been called, perhaps the parents' advocate might feel that he has scored some points for his client. His problem, however, is that his next task is to present his own case, including calling his own clients. Frequently, parents' advocates have the experience of feeling quite satisfied with the progress they have made attacking the local authority's case, only to see all their good work undone when their own clients step into the witness box.

To illustrate how these techniques might be put into effect, some examples of cross-examination exchanges taken from real cases appear in Appendix 6.

FREQUENTLY ASKED QUESTIONS

What if the advocate interrupts me during my answer?
If you look at the judge, the advocate cannot stop you just by using eye contact and body language, so he actually has to speak over you. This looks rude, so is not something he does lightly. It is only likely to happen if you are saying something he does not want you to say or if you are rambling in such a long-winded manner that he speaks for everyone in court in trying to shut you up! Assuming it is not the latter, all the more reason for you to plough on and finish what you have to say – after all, you have sworn to tell the whole truth. If the next question is asked before you have finished, simply complete your answer to the first point before going on to the second.

What if my mind goes blank or I just can't speak?
People sometimes think they will be so frozen with fear that they will be unable to utter a single word. In reality this very rarely happens but even if it does, remember that all your evidence is already before the court in your statements. If you do dry up in the witness box, take a moment to refocus. Remind yourself of the child, who is the reason

you are there. Count to three and look at your statement to refresh your memory. Take a sip of water, take a deep breath, look at the judge and start again.

What if something I say comes out wrong?

Sometimes we get halfway through a sentence and get lost. The best thing to do is stop and start again. If on your mental replay something you have said sounds wrong, or if through a subsequent question it becomes apparent that it has been misunderstood (whether genuinely or deliberately), simply explain to the court that you did not express yourself quite clearly enough and restate what you meant.

I am newly qualified and these are my first care proceedings. Will this be held against me?

This is one of those challenges you can easily anticipate and prepare for. Your qualifications and experience are in your statement so it will be no surprise if the issue is picked up. Don't let it throw you – if your recent qualification is the opposing advocate's best point, he is in trouble! Everyone has to start somewhere and all the professionals in court had a first case once. Having an idea in advance of how to respond will help to give you confidence. For a start, you are qualified – recently or not, you have completed a rigorous course of study. Second, you have the advantage that your knowledge is fresh and up-to-date. Third, you do not work alone – your experience is supplemented by that of your supervisor. You also benefit from input from colleagues from your own and other agencies.

Can the advocate ask me personal questions?

You are there as a professional witness and on the whole the court is unlikely to consider personal questions relevant. If you are asked a personal question, the best course of action is politely to raise the issue with the court, not the advocate, and calmly say that as you are there in a professional capacity, you are not sure of the relevance of your personal circumstances.

However, the very nature of social work is such that sometimes personal questions (like whether you have children yourself) arise in the course of your work with clients. The court might then expect you to answer the question. If your client has never raised the matter with you, you can legitimately point out that it has never been something which has troubled her before in your work together. If, on the other hand, you have discussed this with the client, then you can explain to the court how you dealt with the issue. Some workers are concerned that not having children themselves might be seen as a weakness. In fact, it could be just the opposite, as their knowledge is objective not subjective. Besides which, any professional working with children has experience of a far wider range of children than it would be physically possible for any parent to have.

Remember, though, that evidence is a product of events in a case. If you have confided any personal details to a client, she will tell her solicitor and that information is likely to be thrown back at you in court. If you provide ammunition, don't be surprised if it is fired at you. One social worker sympathised with a client, explaining that she too had been through a messy divorce. It was therefore quite predictable that the advocate challenged her in court as to what right she had to criticise his client's family life when her own life was a mess. If you choose to work in this way, that is a matter for you, but be prepared to find it coming back at you.

There are some pieces of personal information you cannot hide – such as your gender, the colour of your skin, some disabilities, pregnancy or illness (if, for example, you have a lot of sick leave during a case). An advocate might try to argue, for example, that as a white worker you cannot understand the position of his black client, or because you are a woman you have naturally taken the side of the allegedly battered wife against his poor maligned male client. All of these are predictable, if not necessarily very strong, points so you have every opportunity to be prepared for them. The important thing is to keep your cool, explain your objective professionalism and demonstrate it by your reasonable demeanour. You may also wish to acknowledge the client's feelings and tell the court if this is something you have already discussed with her.

What if I am asked for a 'yes' or 'no' answer?

If the answer to the question really is a simple 'yes' or 'no', then do not be afraid to give it. However, in many cases, there are more shades of grey. If the question cannot properly be answered in one word, explain to the court that it is more complicated than the questioner implies and give your fuller answer. Try to avoid saying, 'Yes, but …' as the advocate will leap in as soon as the word 'yes' has crossed your lips and move on to the next question.

What if the advocate keeps asking me what seems like the same question in different ways?

An advocate might use this technique, perhaps to test out the consistency of your answers, especially if he returns to the question after a gap when he has raised other issues. He is unlikely really to expect a professional witness to change her mind or to be inconsistent, but this does sometimes happen with lay witnesses, whereupon, of course, the advocate pounces on any variation or inconsistency. Alternatively, it may be done to unnerve you and make you feel as though you have somehow not given a full or clear enough answer or it might be just to irritate you and make you lose your cool.

All you can do is to keep answering the question and stick to your guns, keeping calm and reasonable at all times. If no one else raises the issue after a while, you might appeal to the court. In one case a psychologist finally said to the judge, 'I really do think I have answered that question', to which the judge said, very emphatically: 'Yes, she has! Several times!'

What if I'm asked a stupid question?

The person asking the question has a right to ask it and is entitled to a response from you. Treat all questions respectfully, whatever you think of them, and do your best to provide an answer. This is especially important for any questions coming from the Bench. One senior social worker was faced with a question from a magistrate which revealed a lack of the most basic understanding of the issues. The social worker rolled her eyes, looked at the ceiling in overt exasperation, sighed and then proceeded to address the Bench as if they were a group of five-year-olds. Everyone else in court felt embarrassed on her behalf. Whatever you say to your team after court in the privacy of your interview room, never reveal your feelings in court and treat every question coming from the Bench as if it is a privilege to respond to such an insightful enquiry.

Can I be asked about other people's evidence?

You can be asked about evidence given by others; for example, to examine contradictions or inconsistencies between witnesses. If you are the key worker, you should already be familiar with all of the evidence submitted. However, if you are a witness giving a discrete piece of evidence, you may not have seen all the evidence before court, so points raised may come as a surprise to you. Usually, the advocate asks the witness to look at and comment on a particular paragraph in another statement. Always take your time to read it carefully, and also read a paragraph or two before and after to get the point into context. In your answer, make sure you stick to what you can legitimately comment on – you cannot say what another witness saw or thought.

What should I call the judges / magistrates?

Magistrates are collectively called 'Your Worships', and the Chair of the Bench is 'Sir' or 'Madam'. A District Judge is 'Sir' or 'Madam', a Circuit Judge is 'Your Honour' and a High Court Judge is 'My Lord/Lady' or 'Your Lordship/Ladyship'. If you can get this right, it adds to your air of professionalism.

One witness knew that she was addressing magistrates, and knew they were 'Your somethings' so came out with 'Your Majesty', which they rather liked! An advocate once went from appearing before magistrates in the morning to a Circuit Judge in the afternoon. He accidentally addressed the judge as 'Your Worships', to which the judge replied 'I don't mind being a worship, but I'm not sure that I want to be plural!' If you cannot remember the right form of address, do not get in a stew – just be respectful and the court is unlikely to mind.

What if I get the giggles?

Laughter in court is generally best avoided – courts deal with very serious matters, and humour is out of place. Never try to make a joke when giving evidence. Advocates also attempt humour at their peril. An advocate acting for a parent once thought it appropriate to tell the Rottweiler joke as part of his closing submissions (Q: What's the difference between a social worker and a Rottweiler? A: You have a chance of getting your child back from a Rottweiler), and was met with a deep glowering silence from the Bench. Very occasionally, a lighter moment occurs, or the judge makes a witty remark, greeted by appreciative simpering from all present, but generally it is best to maintain a serious expression.

Sometimes, though, the very fact that we are involved in a solemn occasion where we know that we are not supposed to laugh makes the urge to do so irresistible, and this is exacerbated by nerves. We all know that dreadful feeling when something that is not at all funny suddenly becomes the most hilarious thing in the world and the more we try to suppress our giggles, the worse it becomes – known as 'corpsing' in the theatrical world. If you feel the urge to laugh welling up inside you, think of something serious, even upsetting, to get you back in balance. Alternatively, focus intensely on a tiny object, such as a speck of dust on a carpet, examine it in minute detail as if meditating to compose yourself. If all else fails, 'accidentally' dropping your pen on the floor gives you an opportunity to hide your face for a moment while you get it back under control.

What if I am sick?

Just having a bit of a cold is not enough to get you out of going to court. If you are genuinely too ill to go, contact your lawyers immediately to discuss what to do – it may, for example, be possible to put your evidence off to another day. You are likely to need a doctor's certificate. It is in fact possible in extreme circumstances for the court to convene around a hospital bed if necessary, so there is no escape.

If you feel ill part way through your evidence, ask for a break, although try to make sure that it does not look like a tactic to avoid difficult questions. On one memorable occasion, when a witness said she felt sick, the judge offered her a bucket!

What if I realise that I know one of the magistrates?

It is crucial to declare this immediately. Justice must not only be done but it must be seen to be done and the court must be utterly impartial. It is possible for the degree of connection between witness and magistrate to be considered. In one case the social worker recognised one of the magistrates as being a member of her choir. Enquiries established that the two women knew each other only by sight, did not know each other's names and had never spoken. All parties were satisfied that the issue had been aired and agreed that the magistrate could continue to sit. Otherwise, she could have stepped down and the court continued with the two remaining magistrates.

*What if there is an important development
in the case the night before court?*

This is not a TV drama, so you cannot save your revelation until you
get into the witness box ('I can now reveal that the abuser is...').
Tell your lawyer immediately, so he can inform the other parties and
everyone can consider their position. It may require the filing of further
evidence, and possibly an adjournment.

*What if I don't personally agree with my
authority's recommendation to the court?*

This is a matter you must deal with long before the case gets to court.
Tell your lawyer straight away so a strategy can be designed. If you
wait until you get into the witness box and you are asked for your own
professional opinion, you have no option but to answer and to get
yourself into all sorts of hot water.

What if there is a break part way through my evidence?

Once you are on oath, you must not discuss the case with anyone until
your evidence is finished. If the court breaks for lunch or adjourns
until another day before you have finished, you must not talk about the
case to anyone unless you have the court's specific permission to do so.
This puts you in a lonely position as, of course, you want to ask how
you are doing, or what you need to emphasise, but you simply cannot.
It is best to stay away from the rest of your team because even if you
studiously discuss nothing but the weather, others seeing you will leap
to the assumption that you are talking about the case.

Chapter 12

After Court

De-briefing

When the case is over, avoid the temptation to breathe a sigh of relief and rush straight back to the pile of other work you have to do. Always build in time for a full de-briefing along with your senior and your legal team to reflect on the outcome, the process and lessons to take forward to the next case. Make sure these lessons are passed on to colleagues in other teams as well as your own – too often, we fail to share useful experience, positive as well as negative. You may find the questionnaire in Appendix 7 helpful.

Witness feedback

Whenever you give evidence, ask for full and honest feedback on how it went. It is quite likely that other people's perceptions will be very different from your own, and social workers often tend to believe that they have performed worse than observers think.

Ask your advocate and any other colleagues who have been in court to give you a detailed review of your evidence – you could ask them to use the witness observation checklist in Appendix 5. If you do not ask, you will not automatically get any feedback at all, especially if you are not the key worker in the case – at most you might receive a standard letter thanking you for coming to court.

Learn from your experience. Build on what went well. Accept praise and acknowledge your strengths – many people perversely seem to find accepting compliments more difficult than hearing criticisms.

Work on the aspects needing improvement. If things did not go as well as you would have liked, consider where the problem really lies. Was it just an off-day? If so, treat it like falling off a horse; you need to get straight back on. The only way of becoming a better witness is through experience. Get stuck back in as soon as you can so you don't have time to build it into a complex, and remember that everyone involved (advocates and judge included) knows what it is like to have a bad day in court – it happens to us all at some time.

Consider whether you could benefit from any mentoring or training on expressing yourself in writing, assertiveness, presentation skills or vocal coaching, or whether you simply need to discuss things with others.

The court's decision

Make sure you properly understand the court's decision – both the full implications of the order itself and the reasons for it. It is quite difficult to take in the full import of a judgment as it goes along, so get a copy of the lay judges' written reasons or a note or official transcript of a judge's decision as soon as possible.

Take the time to read judgments closely and analyse the reasons for the decision with your legal team as there may be significant implications not only for this child and family but for other cases.

In some circumstances it is very important for you to have a copy of the court's order before you leave the building, particularly if you have sought an emergency protection order or recovery order, or in any case where you may swiftly have to show your authority for action.

What if you lose?

By definition, there is a loser in every case; sometimes, although not often, it is the local authority. Of course, it is always disappointing not to get the order you seek – you would not have made the application if you did not genuinely believe it to be the right thing – but your job is only to put the case to the court; it is the court's job to decide.

If the decision goes against your authority, there are effectively two choices – appeal, or live with it. The most important thing at an early stage is to put emotion to one side and look dispassionately at the court's decision with your legal advisers. Has the court really got it wrong – are there grounds for appeal? If so, quick action is required as court rules prescribe tight timescales for entering appeals.

Alternatively, was the case actually more finely balanced? Although the outcome was not your preferred one, is it one which you can understand? Has the court in fact come up with a better solution than the one you were proposing? If so, you need to accept the decision and move on. This of course requires you to reformulate your plans for the child and work with the family; early and anxious consideration within your department is essential.

Put aside any resentment about the decision and work earnestly and optimistically to try to make the court's decision work well for the child and family. As this might mean quite a change of direction, it might be time for a change of worker, without any sense of blame or criticism of the original worker. At the same time, it is worth considering whether your department could have come up with this solution earlier – is there anything to learn for future cases?

The hardest situation to live with is one where the decision went against you and you feel that it's your fault – if only you and/or your team had performed better, the outcome would have been different, and the child is now at continuing risk because of your failure. Natural reactions at this stage might be indulging in 'if only' thinking, blame and recriminations, despair and self-flagellation, denial and deflection or the adoption of an ostrich policy, everyone busying themselves with other things and avoiding the subject. None of these reactions help anybody or achieve anything. Difficult though it may be, what is required is a cool-headed, objective analysis. Even if the situation is not at a level requiring a formal Serious Case Review, you might need to bring in someone who was not directly involved in the case to help with this.

First, it is important to get things into perspective. Don't forget also to consider what went right – even in what feels like a disaster, there are some positives too. When you look at what the problems were, you will probably find that there is no single cause and no single person at fault, but a combination of factors. Don't just consider the court hearing itself – consider the whole process from the social work and inter-agency co-operation before proceedings started right through to the final order. Don't wallow in failure, but turn it round into a positive learning experience. Consider what needs to change for the future, including any strategic issues for the authority. Make sure the whole department learns the lessons – it is no good if one worker or team learns a hard lesson only to have the same mistake repeated by another team in another case. A 'no blame' culture helps people to admit errors and allows everyone to learn from others' mistakes, but unfortunately it seems remarkably challenging for local authorities to embrace such a culture; instead, finger-pointing seems to be a reflex response.

Remember that successful people and organisations are those who learn from setbacks and emerge stronger for the experience.

Success

In the vast majority of cases, Social Services achieve the outcome they seek. If you 'win' your case, there is clearly cause for satisfaction, although triumphalism is never appropriate. Your objective has been achieved and you can proceed immediately to put your plans for the child into practice.

Take as much time to consider a successful outcome as an unsuccessful one. This idea seems to be quite alien to the culture of many local authorities, and although there is an obligation to examine in detail cases which go seriously wrong, there is no expectation that successful cases should be considered in equal detail. This is like trying to learn how to play a game by only studying the losing team's mistakes without even looking at the winners.

Feel free to pat yourself on the back and to take credit when it is due. Your lawyers should ensure that senior members of your department are informed of successful outcomes and any complimentary comments made by the court – often criticisms are passed on but compliments are not. Make sure that any positive lessons learned are shared with colleagues and the department as a whole. There is no point in leaving others to re-invent the wheel when you have already done the job. Share with others news of an impressive barrister, an effective expert or techniques that you found worked well for you. Do your bit to counteract the received wisdom that court work is always a traumatic ordeal.

Dealing with parents

The parents are likely to be in court when the decision is given. Depending on the outcome, they may be angry or distressed. Sometimes they may not understand what the judge says or comprehend its significance. You need to try to anticipate the parents' reactions and give some thought as to how to deal with them including whether, when and how to approach them. Remember that, once the proceedings are over, the court, lawyers and Guardian all fade away, leaving the social worker, family and child to pick up the pieces. It is important for you to consider along with your seniors how to resume work with the child and family after court.

Telling the child

Someone has to tell the child what has happened in court. Who should talk to him and how depends on the child's age, understanding and circumstances. If he has given direct instructions to his solicitor, then that solicitor is the appropriate person to inform him. If not, it may be you or the Guardian, or you may both go to see the child together. In any event, this should be planned in advance. Liaise with the Guardian and child's solicitor and co-ordinate your approach to ensure that the child receives a clear, accurate, age-appropriate and consistent message. It is almost certainly not in his best interests to hear from his parents first, so swift action may be needed.

Conclusion

Only the most difficult, serious and intractable cases culminate in court proceedings. The children before the court are the ones whose cases cause the most anxious concern, so any court work must be given utmost priority.

The court arena may be unfamiliar to you, but, when you understand the context in which you are working and how the system works, there should be no mystique to it. Preparing and presenting cases for court is a skill, and like any other aspect of your professional practice it takes work and improves with experience. Do not expect it to be easy, but equally do not be intimidated.

The court day is not an isolated event but part of a continuum which starts with the work done by you, your colleagues and other agencies with the child and family concerned. Provided that work is sound, the rest of the task centres on presentation, analysis and explanation, first in your statements, then in oral evidence. Preparation is crucial.

Remember that you are not alone; successful court work depends on co-operation and teamwork. Create and maintain close working relationships, especially with your legal team. Make sure you get all the training, advice and support you need.

Once you are in court, never forget that you are there as a professional. The process is not, and must never become, personal. Keep a clear head, and always remember you are there for the child. If you present as a serious, competent, fair and reliable witness, you will earn respect not only for yourself but also your profession.

Preparing and presenting evidence to court is a challenging but necessary step in your professional development as a children and families worker. You chose to work in child protection for a reason. You may sometimes question your own sanity for making that choice, but the chances are that you were motivated by the desire to do good and to protect the weak and vulnerable. That is a noble calling, and should not be forgotten in all the day-to-day difficulties of the work.

As Lord Brown[1] said, 'The well-being of innumerable children up and down the land depends crucially upon...social workers concerned with their safety being subjected by the law to but a single duty: that of safeguarding the child's own welfare'.

That is why you do what you do. And that is why you owe it to yourself, your authority, your profession and, above all, the child, to be well prepared the next time someone says to you 'See you in court!'

---

1   *D v East Berkshire Community Health NHS Trust and others* [2005] 2FLR 284 at p.328 (House of Lords).

Appendix 1

Brief Summary of Key Legal Provisions

The following is a quick reminder of some essential provisions for court work. For fuller information *see* the author's book *A Social Worker's Guide to Children and Families Law*, published by Jessica Kingsley, 2014.

CHILDREN ACT 1989

Welfare principle
s1(1) – when a court considers a child's upbringing, the child's welfare is the court's paramount consideration.

Welfare checklist s1(3)
Factors for the court to consider include:

(a) child's wishes and feelings

(b) child's physical, emotional and educational needs

(c) likely effect of a change in circumstances

(d) age, sex, background and relevant characteristics

(e) harm the child has suffered or is at risk of suffering

(f) capability of parents and relevant others of meeting the child's needs

(g) the range of powers available to the court.

No delay principle s1(2)
The court must bear in mind that, in general, delay is likely to prejudice the child's welfare.

No order principle s1(5)
The court must not make any order unless doing so would be better than making no order.

Grounds for care order – 'threshold criteria'
s31 – a court can only make a care or supervision order if it is satisfied that the child is suffering or is likely to suffer significant harm, and that harm is attributable to the care not being what it would be reasonable to expect a parent to give or to the child being beyond parental control.

'Harm' includes physical, emotional and sexual ill-treatment, impairment of health (physical or mental) or development (intellectual, emotional, social and behavioural) and harm caused by seeing or hearing someone else being ill-treated.

If the threshold criteria are made out, the court goes on to decide what order, if any, to make, considering the welfare principle.

Grounds for interim care order s38
The court can only make an interim case order (ICO) if it is satisfied that there are 'reasonable grounds for believing' that the threshold criteria are made out.

Special guardianship order s14 A–G
There are no specific grounds to prove for a special guardianship roles (SGO); the court decides on the basis of the child's welfare. A special guardian acquires parental responsibility (PR) for the child. The special guardian can act to the exclusion of the others with PR, although they do not lose their PR.

HUMAN RIGHTS ACT 1998
Key articles guaranteed under the Human Rights Act include:

Article 2 – Right to life.

Article 3 – Prohibition against torture and inhuman or degrading treatment or punishment.

Article 6 – Right to a fair trial.

Article 8 – Right to respect for private and family life. Interference with this right can only be justified if it is lawful and is necessary for the protection of the rights of others.

'*Proportionality*' is the principle which means that interference with the right to family life must only go as far as absolutely necessary and no further – it must be proportionate to the need.

ADOPTION AND CHILDREN ACT 2002

Adoption order s46

Adoption transfers the child completely from the birth family to the adoptive family. The child is treated in law as if he had been born into the adoptive family. The adopters acquire full and exclusive PR. Adoption is life-long and irrevocable. The birth parents' PR is terminated and all legal relationships between the child and the entire birth family end.

Placement order (PO) s21 ACA

A PO authorises the local authority to place a child with prospective adopters. A PO must be sought when the care plan in care proceedings is for adoption. Parents must give consent or have it dispensed with on the grounds that they cannot be found, are incapable of giving consent or that the child's welfare 'requires the consent to be dispensed with'.

Statement Checklist

Grade the statement from 1 to 5 where 1 = poor; 2 = needs improvement; 3 = average; 4 = good; 5 = excellent

Layout and structure

Complies with court rules	1	2	3	4	5
Looks attractive and easy to read	1	2	3	4	5
Information accessible and well organised	1	2	3	4	5
Headings and sub-headings well used	1	2	3	4	5
Paragraphs numbered and sensible length	1	2	3	4	5

Statement writer

Clearly identified	1	2	3	4	5
Role clear	1	2	3	4	5
Expertise established	1	2	3	4	5

Language

Plain English used	1	2	3	4	5
Frank but sensitive	1	2	3	4	5
Professional tone	1	2	3	4	5
Correct spelling and grammar	1	2	3	4	5

Content

Clearly gives key information about child and family	1	2	3	4	5
Special needs/cultural issues considered	1	2	3	4	5
Clear illustrative examples given	1	2	3	4	5
Appropriate level of detail	1	2	3	4	5

Right length and not repetitive	1	2	3	4	5
Balanced – addresses both strengths and weaknesses	1	2	3	4	5
Diagrams/exhibits used where helpful	1	2	3	4	5
Showed understanding of relevant law	1	2	3	4	5

Hearsay

Use necessary and justification explained	1	2	3	4	5

Opinions and conclusions

Within writer's expertise	1	2	3	4	5
Drawn from facts	1	2	3	4	5
Clearly explained	1	2	3	4	5
Appropriate reference to legal criteria	1	2	3	4	5

Research/theory

Used only where necessary	1	2	3	4	5
Explained clearly and in context of the case	1	2	3	4	5

Overall

Clear	1	2	3	4	5
Balanced and fair	1	2	3	4	5
Professional and reliable	1	2	3	4	5
Inspires confidence in the writer	1	2	3	4	5
Gives the court the information it needs	1	2	3	4	5

Three words which sum up this statement are:

....

....

....

Template Letter before Proceedings

Reproduced from government guidance 'Court orders and pre-proceedings for local authorities' issued by the Department for Education April 2014.

IMPORTANT!
PLEASE DO NOT IGNORE THIS LETTER – TAKE IT TO A SOLICITOR NOW

Office address contact
Direct line
My ref
Fax
E-mail
Date

SENT BY [HAND/ RECORDED DELIVERY]

Dear [parent and/or full name(s) of all people with parental responsibility]

Re: Insert [name(s) of child(ren)] –

LAST OPPORTUNITY TO STOP YOUR CHILDREN BEING REMOVED FROM YOUR CARE

I am writing to you on behalf of [name of LA] Children's Services.

As you know, [insert name of social worker] has been very concerned about your care of [name(s) of child(ren)] for some time. Things have not improved sufficiently and the situation for your child(ren) has become so serious that we may need to take action.

We are writing to you now to give you a last chance to make the changes to make sure [name(s) of child(ren)] is/are safe. Otherwise we will go to court to ask for them to be removed from your care, if the court decides that is best for them.

We have set out below why we are so concerned about your care of [name(s) of child(ren)] and the things you can and MUST do if you want to avoid us asking the Court to remove them from your care.

HERE ARE OUR MAIN CONCERNS:
[Outline concerns and give examples of when this happened. This should capture ongoing concerns as well as specific concerns]

Date(s) Problem

Date(s) Problem

WHAT YOU MUST DO SO THAT WE WILL NOT GO TO COURT: Come to a meeting with us to talk about these concerns. This meeting will be on [date and time] at the [insert name of office]. The address is [address] and there is a map with this letter to help you find it. At the meeting we will:

- discuss with you what you will need to do to make your child(ren) safe

- discuss with you how we will support you to do this

- discuss with you who in your family could look after your child(ren) if you are not able to, and

- explain what steps we will take if we continue to be worried about [name(s) of child(ren)].

Please contact your social worker on [tel. no.] to tell us if you will come to the meeting.

1. **Get a solicitor:** It is really important that you get advice from a solicitor who specialises in family law as soon as possible. They will help you to understand the situation and advise you about your rights and your options. You also have a right to bring your solicitor with you to the meeting. If you give them this letter you will not have to pay.

    In case you do not have a solicitor, we have sent with this letter a list of local solicitors who work with children and families. They are all separate from Children's Services. You do not have to bring a solicitor to the meeting, but it will be very helpful if you do.

    Information your solicitor will need is: Local authority legal contact: name, address and telephone.

2. **Get your wider family involved:** Our concerns about [name(s) of child(ren)] are very serious. If we do have to go to court and the court decides you cannot care for your child(ren), we will first try and place them with one of your relatives or a person or person(s) close to your child(ren), if it is best for your child(ren) to do this. At the meeting we will discuss with you and your solicitor who might look after your child(ren) if the court decides that it is no longer safe for you to do so.

We look forward to seeing you at the meeting with your solicitor on [date]. If you do not understand any part of this letter, please contact your social worker [name] on [tel. no.]. Please tell your social worker if you need any help with child care or transport arrangements in order to come to the meeting, and we will try to help.

Yours sincerely [name]
Team Manager, Local office/service
Cc: Social worker [name]
Local authority in-house legal team
Enc: Map of office
List of solicitors firms who are members of the Law Society's Children Law Accreditation Scheme.

Public Law Outline Flow Chart[1]

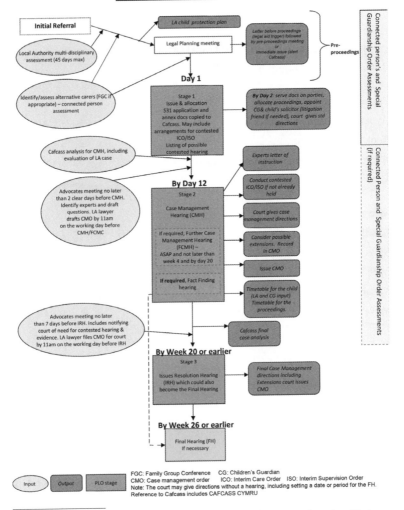

Public Law Outline (26 weeks)

FGC: Family Group Conference   CG: Children's Guardian
CMO: Case management order   ICO: Interim Care Order   ISO: Interim Supervision Order
Note: The court may give directions without a hearing, including setting a date or period for the FH.
Reference to Cafcass includes CAFCASS CYMRU

---

1   Reproduced from www.justice.gov.uk/downloads/protecting-the-vulnerable/care-proceeding-reform/plo-flowchart.pdf

Witness Observation Checklist

Grade the witness from 1 to 5 where 1 = poor; 2 = needs improvement; 3 = average; 4 = good; 5 = excellent

First impressions

Appearance smart and professional	1	2	3	4	5
Took oath confidently	1	2	3	4	5
Addressed judge/magistrates throughout	1	2	3	4	5
Used correct form of address	1	2	3	4	5

Voice

Clearly audible	1	2	3	4	5
Speech easily understood	1	2	3	4	5
Speed well judged	1	2	3	4	5
Variation of pitch and tone	1	2	3	4	5
Voice calm and assured	1	2	3	4	5

Body language

Composed – neither too relaxed nor too tense	1	2	3	4	5
Gestures natural but not excessive	1	2	3	4	5

Language

Used plain English	1	2	3	4	5
Appropriate level of formality	1	2	3	4	5
Respectful	1	2	3	4	5
Frank but sensitive terminology used	1	2	3	4	5

Evidence

Knowledge of case	1	2	3	4	5
Use of own statement/report	1	2	3	4	5

Responses to questions

Listened carefully to questions	1	2	3	4	5
Asked for repeat of questions if necessary	1	2	3	4	5
Took his/her time	1	2	3	4	5
Answered the question actually asked	1	2	3	4	5
Thoughtful and relevant	1	2	3	4	5
Balanced and fair	1	2	3	4	5
Clear and easily comprehensible	1	2	3	4	5
Answers of appropriate length	1	2	3	4	5
Opinions well explained and justified	1	2	3	4	5
Handled challenges well	1	2	3	4	5
Retained composure under pressure	1	2	3	4	5

Overall

Professional, competent and reliable	1	2	3	4	5
Showed awareness of equal opportunities issues	1	2	3	4	5
Inspired confidence	1	2	3	4	5
Gave the court the information it needed	1	2	3	4	5

Three words which sum up this witness are:

. . . .

. . . .

. . . .

Cross-examination Examples

The following examples are all adapted from exchanges between advocate and witness in real care proceedings cases. The advocate's question is followed by the witness's answer in italics.

In each case, consider what the advocate is trying to achieve and what technique he uses to achieve his objective.

How does the witness handle the questioning? Could she have done anything differently? What impression does the court gain following these exchanges?

1. Mother's advocate questioning social worker

My client was always in for your visits, wasn't she?
Yes.

And she always let you in?
Yes.

In fact she was quite welcoming, wasn't she?
Yes.

She let you look around her home.
Yes.

And she always allowed you to see the children.
Yes.

She also attended every session of the assessment, didn't she?
Yes.

So my client has been fully co-operative?
Yes.

Commentary

This line of questioning is delivered in a gentle, unchallenging manner and the social worker probably feels relieved at being asked such simple questions. The advocate emphasises the positive aspects of his client's case, leading the witness with simple closed questions or propositions, to which the witness is invited to agree. The social worker follows where the advocate leads her, and gets into the habit of answering with a simple 'yes'. Although she is happy to accept the propositions, to avoid getting into the rhythm she could change how she expresses her agreement or give more information in response to some questions.

The problem comes with the final question, which takes a much bigger step than the previous ones and represents a conclusion which is not validly drawn from the preceding information. By now the witness is in the habit of agreeing, so does so again. However, she has made the mistake of agreeing to a proposition which she would not have made herself because, although the mother smilingly attended every session, let workers into her house and pleasantly sat while they spoke, she did not actually make any changes or take on board any advice offered. The worker should have considered the last answer more carefully and said something like:

'She is always pleasant and has not been obstructive, but she has not truly co-operated because unfortunately she has not actually made any of the changes we asked her to make.'

As things stand, unless clarification is achieved in re-examination, the advocate has established that the local authority itself says that his client is fully co-operative. He will use this to support his argument that the children can remain at home because clearly his client will co-operate with any services the local authority wishes to put in to protect them.

2. Mother's advocate questioning social worker in first interim hearing in failure to thrive case

How many previous cases of failure to thrive have you handled?
This is the first.

So you have no previous experience whatsoever of such cases?
No, I'm afraid not, but I am supervised by a senior social worker and the community paediatrician advises me.

Perhaps you can tell the court how many previous cases of failure to thrive your supervisor has handled?
I'm afraid I don't know exactly, but he's very experienced.

You can't tell the court whether he has ever handled a case like this before, can you?
Sorry, no, I can't – but I'm sure he must have.

And does the community paediatrician have any special expertise in failure to thrive?
I'm sure she must have, but I don't really know, sorry – you would have to ask her that.

You didn't think to ask her yourself?
No, I didn't, I'm afraid.

So you can't tell the court that anyone responsible for the case has any special experience or expertise in this area!
I don't know the details, I'm afraid, but I'm sure they must have.

Are you aware of the research into techniques of community management of failure to thrive?
No. I'm sorry.

Commentary

The advocate is obviously seeking to cast doubt on the witness's expertise and at the same time to undermine her confidence – and you may feel that he succeeds. These were the first questions in the cross-examination, so the witness started off shakily and her confidence was undermined for the rest of the session. The worker's inability to provide clear information for the court, coupled with her constant apologies, must have left the magistrates wondering how far they could rely on her as a competent professional.

She could have avoided these problems if she had been able, for example, to outline her theoretical understanding of the issue coupled with details of her senior's practical experience – and she could have reminded the court of her own observations of the baby's condition, which in the particular case were such that previous experience was superfluous – it was common sense that something was seriously wrong.

The advocate refers to research. The witness is entitled to ask the court to require him to specify whether he has a particular piece of research in mind. If he proposed to cite this research, he should properly have copied it to other parties in advance. If he has not done so, the witness and her advocate are quite entitled to ask the court for time to read and consider the work he is referring to.

3. Mother's advocate to Children's Guardian supporting an interim care order on a child already voluntarily accommodated in foster care

Why do you support an interim care order?
The local authority needs to share parental responsibility.

But my client has never sought to remove the child from accommodation, has she?
No, she hasn't.

And there is no reason to suppose she might do so in future, is there?
No.

In fact my client has confirmed to you that she accepts the child will remain in foster care for the time being, hasn't she?
Yes, she has.

So an interim care order would add nothing, would it?
It would mean the local authority would share parental responsibility.

On a day-to-day basis precisely what difference would that make?
It would make things more secure, and put the local authority in charge.

Forgive me, I was asking in practical terms on a day-to-day basis, precisely what difference it would make?
The local authority would have parental responsibility and it would secure the child where he is.

The reality is, isn't it, that it you cannot tell the court of one single practical difference it would make, can you! Moving on...

Commentary
In these answers, the Guardian repeats that 'the local authority would have parental responsibility' like a mantra – but it seems she has given little thought to what, if any, real difference it would make. She speaks in generalities and abstractions, when the questions ask for practicalities, so she fails to answer the questions asked, leading to the inference that she has no answer.

Obviously the advocate's questions lead towards submissions on the 'no order' principle and the doctrine of proportionality. He has established that his client has not tried to remove the child, nor is there any suggestion she will do so; she has agreed he will remain in foster care without an order, and no practical reason has been given for an order. Not surprisingly, no order was granted. Never apply for or support an order if you cannot tell the court in plain terms why it is needed.

4. Mother's advocate to social worker in interim care order application

You apply for an interim care order?
Yes, the department's view is that it is now necessary to seek an interim care order with a view to removing the children from home.

Do you agree that children should only be removed from home when absolutely necessary and as a last resort?
Of course.

Do you think that removal is absolutely necessary in this case?
The department takes the view that it is.

I didn't ask what the department thinks. I asked what you think. You are a professional, so what is your own professional opinion?
I have to say that I don't agree that it is necessary.

Commentary
This was a painful personal experience, the recollection of which still causes a shudder, many years later! The social worker and her senior had omitted to tell the legal department that there was a stark difference of professional views and that the key worker disagreed with the application to the court. That same worker was the only witness representing the department in making the application, which, unbeknown to her lawyer, she did not personally support.

The opposing advocate picked up on the worker's consistent reference in her answers to 'the department' and guessed that she was trying to distance herself from the decision. Once the worker was asked the final question, she had little option. She was there as a representative of the department and had made its position clear. However, she was also there as a professional witness and when pressed for her own professional judgment, she clearly could not lie on oath. She therefore gave the only answer she could – to her own lawyer's dismay! You can imagine how far the interim care order application progressed after that.

Court is not the place to tackle professional disagreements. It is neither sensible nor kind to shock your own lawyer in court. If these issues arise, they must be tackled well in advance and in conjunction with your legal team – please!

5. Mother's solicitor to social worker

You complain that my client is rude to you?
That's correct, she does not listen to my advice and is often abusive.

You're newly qualified aren't you?
I have been fully professionally qualified for nine months. I hardly think that's newly qualified, and I have gained considerable experience in that time.

Really? Considerable experience in nine months?
Yes. Absolutely.

You haven't got children yourself have you?
I consider that irrelevant and decline to answer that question.

Even assuming you have some theoretical knowledge, you have no idea what it's like for my client trying to cope on her own with three children under five, do you?
I use the benefit of my professional expertise in working with this mother.

Are you aware that my client finds you unsympathetic and unhelpful?
She has made that perfectly clear many times.

Is it any wonder she sometimes loses her patience and swears at you?
Verbal abuse is not justified whatever her feelings towards me.

Commentary

This advocate clearly knows he cannot refute evidence that his client has failed to co-operate with the social worker and has been abusive to her. His approach is, therefore, to seek to explain his client's actions by showing her feelings about the social worker to be understandable, if not entirely justified. You may consider that the tone of the worker's answers, even referring to 'this mother' rather than using her name, only serves to assist him in this endeavour. If the worker had seemed more understanding of his client's difficulties or shown some empathy towards her, his strategy would have been difficult to sustain. As it is, he is on his way to establishing that the worker is inexperienced, unsympathetic, judgmental and defensive.

He hopes that when his client later gives evidence she will cut a sympathetic figure, preferably apologising for her rudeness to the social worker – then in submissions he will appeal to the Bench effectively saying: 'No wonder things didn't improve – my poor client didn't stand a chance given this obnoxious social worker. She deserves another chance.'

6. Mother's advocate to expert medical witness

Is it possible that the injuries could have been caused by another child?
Well, they were inflicted by someone. It is not possible to determine the age of the perpetrator from the injuries – the only rough guide might come from looking at the force required to cause the injuries. They could have been caused by a child, depending on the age of child you have in mind.

A two-year-old?
Oh no, definitely not! That's simply not possible – only a much older child or an adult could have the strength to inflict injuries of this severity.

Commentary

This advocate's case theory is that the injuries were not caused by his clients but by another child, aged two. However, he overplays his hand. One of the key skills of advocacy is knowing when to stop and to refrain from asking that one question too many. Here, if he had stopped after the first question, his case theory would still be intact – he could tell the court there is an alternative explanation for the injuries, which is plausible because the expert said so. Unfortunately for him, he goes too far and by trying to get the confirmation of the detail of his hypothesis, he succeeds only in destroying it. Sometimes advocates simply get it wrong.

End of Case Questionnaire

Where ratings are suggested from 1 to 5:
1 = poor; 2 = needs improvement; 3 = average; 4 = good; 5 = excellent

Outcome

What was the outcome?

....

....

Was it as expected?   Y / N

Working relationships

How effective was the relationship between social workers   1 2 3 4 5
and legal representatives?

What was the most successful aspect of the relationship?

....

....

What was the least successful?

....

....

How effective was co-operation with other agencies?   1 2 3 4 5

What was the most successful element of co-operation?

....

....

What was the least successful?

....

....

How constructive was the relationship with the Children's   1   2   3   4   5
Guardian?

Why?

. . . .

. . . .

Court procedures

Did case administration work smoothly?   Y / N

Were all court deadlines complied with?   Y / N

If not, where did the problems lie?

. . . .

. . . .

Evidence

How well prepared were the local authority's witness   1   2   3   4   5
statements?

What were their strengths?

. . . .

. . . .

What could be improved upon?

. . . .

. . . .

How effective were the local authority's witnesses in court?   1   2   3   4   5

What were their strengths?

. . . .

. . . .

What could be improved upon?

. . . .

. . . .

Expert

Was the report delivered on time?   Y / N

How useful was it?   1   2   3   4   5

How effective was the expert as a witness in court?   1   2   3   4   5

Would you use this expert again?   Y / N

Give your reasons:

. . . .

. . . .

Advocates

How helpful was the local authority's advocate in conference, case preparation and negotiations?   1   2   3   4   5

How effective was he/she in court?   1   2   3   4   5

Would you use this advocate again?   1   2   3   4   5

Give your reasons:

. . . .

. . . .

Were any of the other advocates impressive?   Y / N

Would you like to instruct them in another case?   Y / N

Overall

What worked well in the case?

. . . .

. . . .

What would you do differently next time?

. . . .

. . . .

What have you learned from the case?

. . . .

. . . .

What lessons from the case (positive messages and/or suggestions for improvement) should be shared with social work or legal colleagues, or with other agencies?

. . . .

. . . .

Index

Statutes and Cases

Index of Statutes

Statutory Instruments

Guidance

The Children Act 1989 Guidance and
Regulations Volume 2: Care Planning,
Placement and Case Review (2010) 72n

Rules and Practice Directions

Family Procedure Rules 2010 71n, 83n, 102,
103, 119r
12A 73n, 119
Practice Direction 22A 84, 85, 87, 89, 90
Practice Direction 25B and Annex 140, 142
Practice Direction 25C, Annex A 142

Index of Cases